"*To Lee Todd for inspiring us to pursue entrepreneurship as a viable career path and nurturing a desire to guide others down that same path. And to Jim Ford, Dave Adkisson, Ashli Watts, Sarah Cathey, and the entire team at the Kentucky Chamber of Commerce for their continued support for our mission to celebrate the most successful entrepreneurs in the Commonwealth of Kentucky.*"

—BRIAN RANEY, AWESOME INC, KENTUCKY
ENTREPRENEUR HALL OF FAME CO-FOUNDER

"*To Matt Dawson, for living WILD.*"

—LUKE MURRAY, AWESOME INC, KENTUCKY
ENTREPRENEUR HALL OF FAME CO-FOUNDER

"*To my children, may you have the courage to take risks.*"

—NICK SUCH, AWESOME INC, KENTUCKY
ENTREPRENEUR HALL OF FAME CO-FOUNDER

UNBRIDLED SPIRIT VOLUME 2

INDUCTION CLASSES 2015–2019

UNBRIDLED
SPIRIT®

LESSONS IN LIFE AND BUSINESS

FROM KENTUCKY'S MOST
SUCCESSFUL ENTREPRENEURS

KENTUCKY ENTREPRENEUR HALL OF FAME

LIONCREST
PUBLISHING

UNBRIDLED SPIRIT VOLUME 2

Lessons in Life and Business from Kentucky's Most Successful Entrepreneurs

FIRST EDITION

ISBN   978-1-5445-3669-9 *Hardcover*

978-1-5445-3670-5 *Paperback*

978-1-5445-3671-2 *Ebook*

CONTENTS

INTRODUCTION

By Luke Murray, Co-founder

It has been five years since I lowered all of the lights in the room, except for those that shone brightly over the wall of photos of the inductees of the Kentucky Entrepreneur Hall of Fame. I sat down underneath it to write an introduction for our first book, *Unbridled Spirit: Lessons in Life and Business from Kentucky's Most Successful Entrepreneurs.*

As I write this next book introduction in 2022, it doesn't feel like much time has passed. But when I stop to think of everything that has happened in my own life, both professionally and personally, it seems like a lifetime ago and I'm not sure I could have gone through it without shared wisdom from those who have gone before me.

When interviewing the entrepreneurs for the second volume of *Unbridled Spirit*, we learned just as valuable of lessons as we did in Volume 1. We also learned some really interesting facts about Kentucky's most famous entrepreneurs.

Who knew that Brown-Forman is the only American spirits company under the same ownership today that existed before, during, and after Prohibition.

Bobby Trussell, the founder of Tempur-Sealey, found out that he left a $50,000 investment check from his uncle on the floor of a Burger King.

R. Dudley Webb purchased an American flag in Jamestown, Kentucky that he flew on the back of his family's boat. That flag became famous when a fireman "borrowed" it and raised it at Ground Zero just after the tragedy of 9/11.

At the peak of her company, Innovative Mattress Solutions, Kim Knopf had 160 retail locations across six states.

After receiving an award at the office Christmas party, Mike Davis told his former boss, "I quit." He realized that the company wouldn't fulfill their end of a deal that they had made.

We were reminded that integrity matters most. When

Jim Headlee chose integrity to honor a customer, he was heavily rewarded when he coincidently ran into that same customer twelve years later.

And finally, as Jess Correll mentors young founders, he tells them, "Do what you say you're going to do every time. Even when it's hard, especially when it's hard. Be a person of integrity."

However, the most important lesson that we learned: we need examples of entrepreneurship in order to be successful ourselves. Starting a business is one of the most complicated puzzles you'll ever have to complete. When you get any puzzle out of the box, your goal is to have all of the pieces come together to form the beautiful portrait intended by the creator of the puzzle. But if you've ever tried completing a puzzle without the picture on the box, you learned it's pretty much impossible. The picture, serving as the example solution of the final product, is critical to successfully completing any puzzle.

In 2018, Brian (my co-founder) and his wife decided to foster kids and he became a dad (and grandad) to three girls all in the same day—ask him about it sometime. Initially, he would tell you that he was clueless as to how to solve the puzzle of raising three girls.

But he was confident he would be a good dad because he

had a great example. His dad and many other men in his life provided pictures of what a good father looked like.

As an entrepreneur, our journey is the same. It often starts off looking like the pieces of a complex puzzle scattered on a table. Luckily, the entrepreneurs in this book generously offer their stories as a picture to guide us. And having that picture makes putting the puzzle pieces of entrepreneurship together seem much more possible.

The Kentucky Entrepreneur Hall of Fame exists, in part, to inspire others to pursue similarly ambitious endeavors to those its inductees are known most widely for. As a co-founder of the Hall of Fame and an entrepreneur myself, I am proud of the Hall of Fame's impact and I am also proud to be my own customer.

The entrepreneurs in the Kentucky Entrepreneur Hall of Fame have modeled many of the decisions we've made since publishing our last book. It's our hope that these stories will help you assemble your entrepreneurial puzzle as well.

LUKE MURRAY, KENTUCKY ENTREPRENEUR
HALL OF FAME CO-FOUNDER

WRITTEN AT AWESOME INC IN LEXINGTON, KENTUCKY
JUNE 24, 2022

PART 1

2015 INDUCTEES: GEORGE GARVIN BROWN, PHIL GREER, JIM PATTERSON, AND JAMES THORNTON

GEORGE GARVIN BROWN

Honorary recollection by Marshall Farrar, George Garvin Brown's Great-Great-Grandson.

* Images provided by Brown-Forman archives.

In 1846, George Garvin Brown was born in Munfordville, Kentucky. Although little is known of his upbringing, history tells us that George found his way to Louisville as a young adult. There, he teamed up with his half brother, John Thompson Street Brown, to form a business originally called J. T. S. Brown & Brother.

Established in 1870, the partnership was the first distillery to sell whiskey in a sealed glass bottle, which ensured a consistently high-quality product. These two admirable traits would become signature characteristics of the brand founded by George Garvin Brown.

The brothers split ways about three years later. After almost two decades and a series of other partnerships, George partnered with his longtime friend and accountant, George Forman. Thus, in 1890, the new partnership formed the company name that still stands today—Brown-Forman.

More than a century and a half have passed since George Garvin Brown began his entrepreneurial journey. However, a quick glance into his history shows that he was a business-person quite far ahead of his time.

Most people don't think of innovation when it comes to the whiskey and fine spirits business, but George Garvin Brown was perhaps the greatest innovator in the history of the industry. George had an entrepreneurial spirit in his DNA, and it suited him well in separating his brand from all the disreputable distilleries and unbranded competition of that time period.

INTEGRITY AS A SIGNATURE SELLING POINT

Transport yourself to 1870. The country had just gotten through the Civil War, so change was happening every-where. People were looking to heal their physical and emotional scars, also seeking change and integrity from their fellow citizens.

Life had been turned upside-down for so many years that most of the country's population wanted nothing more than to get back to normal. In post-Civil War Louisville (where George had taken roots), people were looking for products and services they could count on. Businesses were popping up all along the Ohio River, but nobody was sure who they could trust. The fine spirits industry was no different. Although people had been making whiskey for multiple generations, the quality varied greatly from one provider to the next and even from one barrel to the next. Responsible consumers had no idea which product would provide them the benefit for which they were looking.

At the time, people drank whiskey for two reasons: one was today's more commonly known and accepted practice as a leisure pastime. The other was for medicinal purposes. Doctors who were forming practices all over the country prescribed whiskey for various ailments: from pain to mental health and almost anything in between. With whiskey in high demand, George Garvin Brown spotted the opportunity to give the people what they wanted in his product, which was consistency above all else.

By batching and bottling his whiskey with the same high-quality standards every time, George guaranteed that the consumer would have their expectations of his whiskey satisfied in every bottle. Today's consumer takes that sort of thing for granted. For example, when customers open a bag of Lay's potato chips today, they expect a certain consistent quality. In 1870, however, this was a novel idea.

Disreputable brewers were using cheaper ingredients to produce low-quality brands, and others were making whiskey that was passable in some bottles but virtually undrinkable in others. The idea of consistently high-quality whiskey in *every* bottle of Old Forester, which is the brand he made famous, was so innovative that it earned him a stellar reputation in the community. George proved his integrity by paying bank loans in a timely manner. He even paid back a debt from which he had been relieved of the obligation to pay, which earned him an Integrity Cup. Quickly, George Garvin Brown became known as a man of character and values that made him one of Kentucky's most successful entrepreneurs of all time.

OVERCOMING SEEMINGLY INSURMOUNTABLE ADVERSITY

After using his stellar reputation as an honest businessperson with an excellent product, George incorporated the business and purchased one of his suppliers—the B. F. Mattingly Distillery in St. Mary's, Kentucky. That site became Brown-Forman's first location for distilling operations.

In 1904, George's son Owsley joined the business and took over a leadership role when George passed away thirteen years later. That handoff in 1917, from father to son, represented the first generational torch-passing of the company's legacy. Since then, the family ties in the business have remained strong throughout four more generations (and counting).

Before George's passing, he must have sensed the winds of change blowing in an unfavorable and alarming direction for the industry. Murmurings that alcoholic beverages would soon be classified as illegal were beginning to surface, and George took an active stance in fighting the injustice to his industry. In 1910, he vigilantly and convincingly wrote a book titled, *The Holy Bible Repudiates Prohibition*. Throughout its pages, he mentions how often the Good Book promotes the responsible consumption of alcohol. As a man with strong religious beliefs, the impact of his words were extremely enlightening for those who read the work.

Only three years after his father's passing, the company's new leader, Owsley Brown, was faced with the biggest obstacle of Brown-Forman's storied history—Prohibition. The idea of an entrepreneur's product being deemed illegal may seem insurmountable to some but not to the Brown family legacy. Following in his father's footsteps of being an innovator, Owsley Brown argued that the company's product should be used as a medicinal aid. The US government agreed and granted Brown-Forman and many other distillers permission to bottle medicinal whiskey. Brown-Forman is the *only* American spirits company under the same ownership today that existed before, during, and after Prohibition.

While keeping the company operational, Brown-Forman consolidated all operations at 1908 Howard Street in Louisville with the purchase of the G. Lee Redmon Company and its warehouses. Almost a hundred years later, the site is still the company's center of operations. Some renovations have occurred, but the jobs and high-quality products remain in place.

WHERE IS BROWN-FORMAN TODAY?

The company didn't make much money for the thirteen years that Prohibition lasted, but it stayed afloat. Shortly after Prohibition ended in 1933, the company went public. Old Forester grew to become one of the most reputable and popular brands in the area. Soon enough, it was distributed well beyond Louisville.

From 1933 to about 1965, tremendous growth occurred in the industry. Leadership at Brown-Forman recognized the upward trend and invested heavily with acquisitions such as Jack Daniels, Southern Comfort, Canadian Mist, and others.

After the industry boom, the company had to pivot as it faced a glut of suppliers and a resulting reduction in demand. With the state of the industry being a little over-run by smaller competitors, Brown-Forman diversified into other products including wine, tequila, vodka, gin, and liquor.

Most recently, there has been more of a focus on the core competencies of the company, which are whiskey and pre-mium spirits, but all of Brown-Forman's products represent a part of the company's commitment to *demonstrate and ensure there is nothing better in the market today.*

The company is still family-oriented with the sixth gen-eration currently working in the business. It is also proud to employ over 5,200 people, about 1,300 of them at its headquarters located in Louisville. All of this is thanks to a nineteenth-century entrepreneur with the novel idea to produce a consistently high-quality product and establish an excellent business reputation. If only all brands adhered to such values and guidance.

A SPECIAL THANKS

So many times in an entrepreneurial journey, a support-ive spouse is behind the success. This is definitely true in the case of George Garvin Brown. His wife of many years, Amelia Bryant Owsley, was highly impactful in his success.

The couple married in 1876. From letters that have surfaced, George leaned on his wife as a partner in his decision making for the business quite often. In addition to Owsley, the couple also had a boy named Robinson.

When a business runs six generations deep, a strong sense of family must have been at its roots. This is definitely the case when it comes to the Brown-Forman company. George was a family man through the core of his being. He was also a man of strong faith and one who believed deeply in community.

Undoubtedly, George would thank his wife, two children, and the following generations who have continued his esteemed legacy by growing the company to where it stands today.

HIS ADVICE

From the history of George Garvin Brown, it's easy to identify integrity as his signature for success. *By insisting on quality and consistency above all else, George instilled an unparalleled faith in his brand. Integrity became his greatest asset, and he would likely espouse the same virtue for today's aspiring entrepreneurs.* George always led his business from a standpoint of authenticity. We can all learn a great lesson from that.

Awesome Inc and the Kentucky Entrepreneur Hall of Fame salute George Garvin Brown for his contributions as an innovator and the example he set for the entrepreneurial community.

"By insisting on quality and consistency above all else, George instilled an unparalleled faith in his brand. Integrity became his greatest asset, and he would likely espouse the same virtue for today's aspiring entrepreneurs."

PHIL GREER

I grew up in the small coal-mining town of Jenkins, Kentucky, which is part of Letcher County, situated on the south-central border of Virginia.

Thinking back to my childhood, I was just about the happiest kid on the planet. I played Little League baseball, football, basketball, and went squirrel hunting after school.

My mom was an intelligent person who loved and cared for me, my younger brother, and my younger sister. Our family upheld the typical American values of those days. We had a humble home with plenty of good food to eat and clothes to wear. In our early years, my siblings and I were taught to behave properly and respect authority, mostly by my dad who was a highly decorated World War II hero and the disciplinarian in our family.

I was never a great student, but I managed to get by. Fortunately, I was good enough at athletics to earn a football scholarship to attend the University of Kentucky (UK).

As the son of a coal miner, I learned the precious value of a dollar early in life. For my first two years at UK, I did not have the luxury of an automobile to take me home and back for breaks. Without reliable transportation, I hitchhiked back and forth until my junior year, when I made just enough money to buy an old, beat-up jalopy that could get me where I needed to go...barely.

At first, hitchhiking was a long process because almost nobody wanted to pick up a stranger wandering his way down the side of a road. Although that was probably a smart choice, it took me forever to get home and back to school that way. It seemed like hundreds of cars would pass me by, maybe more, before someone would finally pull over and give me a ride.

That all changed when I got my first letter jacket for lettering on the football team. There are so many UK fans out there, just about every car would stop to pick me up when they saw the blue-and-white Wildcats jacket.

As a freshman, I was part of the infamous Thin Thirty coached by Charlie Bradshaw. Coach Bradshaw was a little gruff; actually, some folks might have called him a madman. In 1962, the team was known as the Thin Thirty because we started the season with eighty-eight players and finished the year with just thirty. With his in-your-face style, Coach Bradshaw drove away more than half the team that year. I stuck with it, however, as I've never been afraid of adversity. Later in life, this trait likely served me quite well as an entrepreneur.

MY PASSION FOR TEACHING AND COACHING

After playing college football for five years, I graduated from UK with a bachelor's degree in health, physical education, and recreation. Not long after, Roy Walton, who previously brought me on as a student teacher, hired me as an assistant coach for Tates Creek High School's football program in Lexington. Roy was a famous coach in the area. Our 1972 team went undefeated (and I'm about to attend the fiftieth reunion of that team).

I spent seventeen years as a physical education teacher and coach of football, women's tennis, and wrestling at Tates Creek. Football was a little more my style and our women's tennis team was spectacular. I'm not sure if we lost a match the whole time I was there. The funny thing is that

I had almost nothing to do with their success. I was just lucky enough to walk into a situation where the girls were world-class tennis players. One of those girls even went on to play in Wimbledon.

WORKING HARD AND MAKING THE MOST OF MY OPPORTUNITIES

Coaching is what ultimately got me started on the road to entrepreneurship. A fellow coach at Tates Creek, Dave Bunnell, convinced me to take the real estate broker's test and we started a real estate company together, Bunnell Greer Realtors.

Dave and I worked hard in the real estate game, and I continued to work almost any job I could to make money for a while. I taught physical education at the high school; I refereed Southeastern Conference college basketball games; I drove a freight truck a couple of nights a week. I also worked as a construction laborer for Roy Walton during the summer.

Not too long after I got my real estate license, I caught my first big break. There was a woman who owned a farm with about forty acres of land in town. I had started to learn a little about real estate and figured there might be some value in owning that piece of property. Until that point, I had never really thought about borrowing a multimillion-dollar loan, but I thought this might be worth the risk.

I walked up to her property, knocked on the door, and she answered. Through the screen door, she hollered at me, "If you're a real estate person, get off my porch!"

Obviously, I wasn't going to make any progress by just talking to her, so I left. But I didn't give up. Instead, I went down the street, bought a big box of candy and flowers, and returned. I knocked on her door again, and this time, she let me in.

On her mantel, she had a big glass fishbowl half-full with cards from real estate agents. One look at that and I knew I had plenty of competition. So I built a relationship with her. She was getting along in years, and I knew in those days that elderly people appreciated folks who dressed nice. So I made it a point to wear nice clothes and go have a chat with this nice lady just about every week. One day, I said, "I want to buy your farm."

She asked me, "How much would you give me for it?"

I said, "Ma'am, I want to know what it's worth. You tell me."

She threw out her asking price. At the time, that was the highest price per acre for any farm in the area. I said, "Well, I'll take it!"

My next step was to get financing through a bank, bring her

a contract, and get the deal signed. Three weeks later, the farm was mine. Within a month, a business from St. Louis approached me to buy it for a nice profit.

Some good luck may have shined upon me with that deal, but it's not like I didn't work hard at it. I've always worked hard. That deal just gave me the kickstart I needed to grow as an entrepreneur.

Unfortunately, my partner, Dave Bunnell, encountered some health problems and left the real estate business. That's when Craig Dunn took over as my partner. Bunnell Greer Realtors officially became Dunn Greer Realtors. The business was going well at the time, but Craig's hard work made it even more prosperous. Shortly after the success we built there, I transitioned into a full-time business owner and started Greer Companies.

BUILDING PROSPERITY

I worked hard while getting Greer Companies off the ground, probably a little too hard. We built a lot of houses and commercial properties in those days, and I did most of the work myself.

Eventually, I and the other people who worked closely with me decided to jump into the restaurant business. In 1989, we built and opened our first Shoney's. At one time, we owned five or six of them.

Our business approach at the time wasn't all that refined. We learned things the hard way, but we could also outwork just about anybody. So some ideas worked out great, while others, not quite as well. Either way, it was full speed ahead at all times, and we learned from our mistakes. Truthfully, I'm not sure how we made it from those early days, but we worked hard and believed in ourselves.

With faith in our ability and a never-ending work ethic, we ventured into another restaurant chain, Fazoli's, in 1994. And a couple of years later, in 1996, Greer Companies opened its first Cheddar's.

As Greer Companies dived deeper into the hospitality and commercial real estate development industry, my son, Lee, graduated from the University of Virginia. After working in New York for a brief period of time, he decided to come home and help me grow our involvement with the Cheddar's franchise.

Cheddar's was the restaurant that took Greer Companies to the next level of prosperity. While I focused on building the locations, an investor, Steve Pottinger, and my son, Lee, kept a close eye on operations. That proved to be the dream team, and banks began loaning us money whenever we asked for it.

We built and operated forty-five Cheddar's restaurants at our peak investment. Each of the sites was carefully selected, and we built beautiful buildings—places where families would want to come in, sit down, and share a meal together. Greer Companies was on top of the world because of hard work, a belief in ourselves, and the discovery of a great opportunity like Cheddar's.

NEGOTIATING THE SALE AS A FRANCHISEE

After a while, it became increasingly difficult to find good help. We also had a lot of assets tied up in the banks, so we figured it might be a good time to sell. However, a problem surfaced in our franchise agreement, which was that we had signed what's called a first right of refusal.

The first step for us to sell was to find out if Cheddar's would pay us full price for the value of our forty-five locations. They were not interested in doing that, so our next step was to look for a potential buyer.

Luckily, I had a friend in Florida who loved the Cheddar's brand, so he wanted to get in as soon as I approached him with the idea. However, it wasn't going to be as simple as signing on the dotted line. Whatever purchase price we agreed on had to be presented to Cheddar's first. If they exercised their option to buy, my buyer would be out of the deal. His time and resources invested to that point would also be lost. So I made a deal with him. I told him if Cheddar's exercised their option to buy, I would pay him $1 million as a breakup fee.

We thought that Cheddar's would step up to the plate when we found a legitimate buyer, and we were correct. The parent company agreed to buy our locations, and I paid my friend the $1 million he was owed. Overall, I would say we all came out of that deal in great shape!

A SPECIAL THANKS

As of 2022, I still run Greer Companies and I don't operate any differently now than I did ten years ago. I still go to the office happy every day because I've been so fortunate to work with great people and achieve just about anything I ever wanted out of my entrepreneurial endeavors. The focus of the business now is a little more on small properties and shopping centers, but we have an accounting firm that takes care of collecting the rent and making sure our books are healthy.

The biggest reason for my success is my wife, Mary. She stuck by me through the good times and the bad. I wasn't home much while growing Greer Companies to what it is today, but I was always fortunate to have a wife and family who supported me the whole time. Balancing business with family was hard, but family is more important, so I always tried to attend as many cheerleading contests, football games, baseball games, and other family events as I possibly could.

In addition to my son, Lee, I have twin daughters, Kelli and Kristen. All of them have become successful in their own ways. Lee, of course, has been an integral part of Greer Companies for over twenty years now. One of my daughters, Kristen Greer, is a businessperson in New York, and the other, Kelli Webb, is a doctor.

Life has blessed me with a supportive and successful family. My biggest thanks of all go to my wife, Mary, and my kids, Lee, Kelli, and Kristen: I couldn't have done it without you.

MY ADVICE

One last thing. If you're an aspiring Kentucky entrepreneur, remember this: *If you think you can, you can.* I would wager that nobody expected the son of a coal miner from Jenkins, Kentucky could be where I am today, but I did it because I always believed I could; you can if you think you can.

"If you think you can, you can."

JIM PATTERSON

 I was born in 1933 and grew up in one of the more destitute sections of Louisville. Our family was poor, but we didn't realize it because it was all we knew. We lived in a shotgun house, which was a popular style of home for those days. A shotgun house is a rectangular building about twelve feet wide with rooms that run back to front. Ours had four rooms total, but no bathroom. Like I said, it was all we knew, but I still had hopes that someday I would find a way out of that neighborhood.

Fortunately, I was a good athlete in my younger days, playing mostly football and baseball. Playing baseball in high school proved to be my ticket out of that downtrodden neighborhood, as I was awarded a scholarship to play at the University of Louisville (UofL).

College was an interesting experience for me because I never cared much about my classes; I was too busy working three jobs. By the time I was nineteen years old, I was already selling insurance. This was around 1954, and I made about $15,000 that year (pretty good money for those days, especially for a college kid who was also playing baseball and taking classes).

One thing became abundantly clear when I was selling insurance: just about every person who had enough money to buy a policy from me was a business owner. That left a tremendous impression on me.

GETTING STARTED WITH JERRY'S

When I graduated from UofL, all I could think about was starting my own business. I remembered all those insurance customers who seemed to be making a lot of money on their own, so I started thinking about different opportunities around me.

I heard that drive-in restaurants were making a lot of money, so I reached out to the owner of a local franchise called Jerry's; his name was Warren Rosenthal. These were the days of carhops, where people would drive up to a speaker system, place their order, and have their food delivered to their car. Jerry's was a franchise that exemplified that carhop business model.

After a bit of talking, we determined that Hick's, a famous old Louisville dining institution that had closed, might make a good spot for a Jerry's franchise. With Warren's help, I leased the location, remodeled from the ground up, and opened my first Jerry's drive-in restaurant there in 1959.

Business struggled for the first couple of years, as I quickly found out that I knew little about running a restaurant. I realized there's no better teacher than experience, so I set out to learn as much as I could from my mistakes. After giving myself some time to grow and with the eventual success of my first location, I decided to open two more restaurants in Bowling Green, which both found success much more quickly than the first.

THE EVENT THAT BOOSTED MY ENTREPRENEURIAL JOURNEY

With the three Jerry's franchises up and running, I had started to make real money for the first time in my life. Things were going well, and I knew I was growing as an entrepreneur. Around this time, Warren Rosenthal invited me to join him for a conference at Harvard University. I never considered myself a Harvard man, but I also never let a good opportunity pass me by, so I went to this five-day conference anyway.

When that conference started, I hid in the back of the room, feeling like I didn't belong there. However, I was quickly drawn in by the case studies they presented. The material seemed to be easily applicable and made a lot of sense. By the last day, I sat in the front and was convinced I could do something special in the business world. That was the moment it all came together for me.

Shortly after that conference, I visited Houston with a friend. I had heard a lot of rumblings about fish and chips, so we decided to take a look at a local spot called Alfie's Fish & Chips.

LONG JOHN SILVER'S BEGINS

The restaurant was in a poor section of the city, reminding me of where I grew up, but the product struck me as something with a lot of potential. Until then, I associated eating fish with having to deal with bones and the unpleasant smell of cod liver oil. There was no such thing as frozen food in the 1940s...at least not where I lived.

I was amazed when I sampled the delicious, bone-free cod. The idea of eating fish like it was a boneless breast of chicken had such a lasting impact on me that I knew there was potential in opening this type of restaurant in Kentucky.

At the end of our visit, the owner of Alfie's approached me.

My heart raced as he said, "You know, I can sell you a franchise whenever you want one."

When I got back to Louisville, I contacted Warren Rosenthal, told him about my experience with those fish and chips, and explained that there was a big opportunity in buying a franchise locally and expanding it. There was one problem: in those days, restricted franchise contracts were commonplace, meaning I couldn't do anything about buying another restaurant without Warren's permission. Fortunately, he was quite amenable to the idea. He said, "Why don't we do it together?"

I asked him, "Well, how do you want to do it, then?"

Warren told me, "60-40 sounds right."

I said, "Are you sure that 40 percent is enough for you?"

He responded, "No, it's not. Forty is your number."

Again, I was no Harvard man, but I understood that sixty was more than forty. Regardless, I accepted the lower number as an opportunity to do something big. After all, forty is bigger than zero. We came to an agreement, and I moved to Lexington to begin planning for the restaurant chain that would become Long John Silver's in 1969.

A NEW BEGINNING

I sold my Jerry's restaurants and wrote a check for $40,000 for the new investment in Long John Silver's. I remember saying to myself, "One day, I hope this will be worth something." Five years later, I got back $20 million for that investment. Later, after Warren and I had a disagreement that couldn't be resolved, I was fired from Long John Silver's in 1975, followed by negotiations for the value of the original 40 percent that I put into the business.

At its peak, Long John Silver's had over 1,300 locations and employed over 8,400 workers. I don't know where the numbers stand for that franchise today, but I was the co-founder and a major decision maker in getting that business built, scaled, and running at peak performance.

When I was terminated from Long John Silver's, I was in a scary position. I was forty-one years old with no job and no business. I did, however, have my integrity, mental fortitude, and drive to succeed firmly intact. As is often the case for entrepreneurs, it all worked out in the end.

That same year that I was let go, I took a shot at the oil and gas business, where I had the misfortune of immediately owning two or three successful oil wells. That may have provided me with a false sense of optimism because the next dozen or so came up dry. Still, I learned a lot about the industry. Overall, my company, Gulfstream Petroleum, in Houston, Texas had reasonable success.

While operating that business in Houston, a local Mexican restaurant caught my eye. They were doing about $3 million per year, which impressed me, to say the least. At the time, there were few, if any, Mexican restaurants in Louisville. So I got involved with Chi-Chi's around 1982 as an early investor with a franchisee who opened several successful locations in the Louisville area. By the time Chi-Chi's went public, I was a large shareholder, pleased with my investment.

In 1988, we merged with another Mexican restaurant company, and I was already beginning to look for my next restaurant venture. Around that time, some colleagues told me about an idea they had for a double drive-thru restaurant. The thought made sense to me because I had heard a lot of positive buzz about In-N-Out Burger in California. I decided to back those people, but they didn't really know anything about the business. All they had was a great name—Rally's.

We brought in some partners for Rally's, and in 1989, we took that business public as well. Unfortunately, the partners in Rally's didn't see eye to eye often enough for the business to prosper as much as I would have hoped, so I got out of that situation in the early 1990s.

ANOTHER NEW BEGINNING

Resiliency is a big part of entrepreneurship. The dissolution of my involvement with the Rally's franchise left me in a position similar to where I was after being released from my ownership in Long John Silver's. This time, I rebounded with much greater success.

Several restaurant partners and I operated Wendy's restaurants for a number of years, attaining tremendous success. Just about all of them became millionaires. Being a millionaire today doesn't mean what it did in those days, but we all enjoyed a good life, free from financial worry, from that point on. Overall, we owned and operated a total of forty-seven Wendy's locations. I'm still a partner in that venture today. Although that was likely the most lucrative business move I ever made, my entrepreneurial journey was not done.

Toward the end of the 1990s, I had an opportunity to start a property and casualty company in Florida. A few years later, we started a surety business. As the 2000s unfolded, we sold both of those entities at a good profit. Most recently, we began a franchise called Blaze Pizza, which has also become a successful venture.

Today, I look back on the many hills and valleys of my time in the business world. I would say it's been a good life and I have many special people to thank for having believed in me, supported me, and played a major role in my success.

A SPECIAL THANKS

Even though our relationship ended with my dismissal from the Jerry's franchise, Warren Rosenthal is probably still the greatest mentor I've had in my business life. We were close friends for a long time and we made a great business team.

I'll never forget that Warren was generous enough to invite me to that conference at Harvard when I only represented a small company. The rest of the attendees were presidents and vice presidents of much larger, publicly held businesses. That five-day event changed my life. It helped me to see what was possible. Sure, I felt out of place at first, but I walked out of that event with the inspiration and motivation to dream big, take action, and have a serious impact in the business world.

MY ADVICE

Today, I'm eternally grateful for others who have supported me on my entrepreneurial journey. My wife, Dot, has been the driving force behind my career since I graduated from UofL many years ago.

I've always considered my work to be a family business, as my oldest daughter, Deborah, and son, Jim, have been involved with the business for many years now. We also have a second daughter, Sharon, whom I'm equally proud of.

If you're reading this with any aspirations of your own to become an entrepreneur and make a difference in the world, I would say it's important to have unquestioned integrity. Be honest and follow through, while keeping your eye open for every opportunity that comes your way. Most importantly, I would say, *"Treasure your integrity, because you can only lose it once."*

"Treasure your integrity, because you can only lose it once."

JAMES THORNTON

Honorary recollection by James's son, Matt Thornton.

Although James "Jim" Thornton was born in Lebanon, Kentucky in 1927, his family didn't live there long enough for James to ever know it as home. They moved many times while he was still young, going from one Depression-era community to another until they settled in Southern Indiana, just across the bridge from Louisville, Kentucky. From those humble beginnings, Jim grew up with a strong will and an early desire to achieve more.

After a middle school education, Jim became convinced that school wasn't for him, often joking about how proud he was to have made it all the way through eighth grade. Although Mom and Stepdad were not keen on the idea of Jim quitting school, the opportunities awaiting him in this wide world were far too appealing for him to put off any longer.

When examining Jim's early handwritten notes to colleagues and family, it's possible that he might have been severely dyslexic and undiagnosed, which greatly hampered his ability to succeed in school. Language and reading were a struggle, but many people who worked with him said the man was a human calculator, as math was never a problem. In fact, it was a gift. Jim could solve complex business equations with nothing more than a fifteen-second ponderance.

EARLY ENTREPRENEURIAL ENDEAVORS

Despite his parents' objections, Jim went on to his first entrepreneurial endeavor at the age of fourteen. When most kids were in school, Jim managed to avoid the truancy officer and hitchhiked to Kansas so he could drive gravel trucks for some quick cash. Not only was he supposed to be in school, but he did not have a driver's license.

Jim was one of four kids in one room of his parents' home, so everybody had to pitch in when possible. Of course, he also had bigger ideas in mind.

Two years later, Jim was sixteen and had gathered enough money to open his first gas station. It wasn't anything like the stations we use today. The station consisted of nothing more than an above-ground tank, a pump, and a semicircle carved out of the side of the road for access and exit. The restrictions of today's business codes would never allow for something like that today, but in those days, a sixteen-year-old kid with a relentless work ethic and a little chutzpah could more easily get started on fulfilling his dream.

PRODUCTIVE PARTNERSHIPS

Not long after opening that first station, Jim partnered with two men—Gilbert Dance and Albert Mallory. Interestingly enough, Dance would later become his father-in-law. The trio of entrepreneurs then ventured into the opening of several Dixie Dance gas stations until Jim broke away from the partnership and opened his own station again around 1952, which led to another joint venture.

This time, Jim partnered with Ashland Oil. Over the next decade and a half, the ownership expanded to operate over 150 Payless Stations, across twenty-two states in the Southeast and Midwest sections of the country. In 1966, Jim sold his interest to Ashland Oil but remained a board member until 1971. Those stations became SuperAmerica stores and are now the Speedway stores that so many of us visit on a regular basis.

After selling his interest in the company, Jim could have stayed out of the operations aspect of the business and remained a board member for the rest of his life. However, he was only in his mid-forties at the time and that lifestyle didn't suit his personality well. In fact, Jim referred to his time spent on that board as "a slow and deliberate march toward insanity."

Fortunately, this was before the confounding legalese of noncompete agreements, so Jim and the board knew they were able to part ways in a way where both parties felt reasonably compensated. The deal stated that Jim would retake ownership of a few stations and step away from the board permanently.

In 1971, Jim took back the stations that were agreed upon, hired back some of his best employees, and founded Thornton Oil.

THE EVOLUTION OF THORNTON'S

Jim's solo venture began as predominantly a service station selling gasoline with a few extras like cigarettes and quarts of oil. In the 1980s, however, a new type of service state had emerged. The convenience store had arrived and wasn't going anywhere.

At this point, Thornton Oil had reached around seventeen

states. With the understanding that the convenience store format was going to be crucial to the long-term viability of the company, Thornton Oil had to restructure its business model.

A lot of complexity existed around the convenience store format—so much that Jim knew it would be difficult to effectively manage numerous stores scattered across several states. He determined that the company needed to entrench itself within its roots of Louisville, Kentucky and rebuild from there with the convenience store as part of its service offering. This was the beginning of the Thornton's brand.

With that new business model, Thornton's rebuilt to forty units within two years. Eventually, the business expanded to around 200 stores in several states once again.

Jim maintained an active role in the business until the age of ninety-two. Those closest to him said that he was their best business analyst even in his nineties, working three days a week and religiously poring over the company's profit and loss (P&L) statements. Every month, he would read through it, line by line for all of their stores, circling everything he didn't like in red and placing a checkmark next to everything he liked in blue. A simple yet perfect system.

In 1994, his son Matthew joined the company and was promoted to Chief Executive Officer (CEO) in 2001. Matthew remained in that role until 2018 when the business was sold to BP.

Jim's entrepreneurial fire never dissipated. He pursued investments in lumber mills, hotels, restaurants, racetracks, and real estate development during the years of prosperity with Thornton's. His favorite business, however, was always the gas station because it produced cash, whereas a lot of those other ventures didn't. Thornton's grew to generate more than $2.3 billion in annual revenue and at one time was ranked 250th in *Forbes* magazine's annual list of 500 largest privately held companies in the country. Not bad for a kid with an eighth-grade education.

A SPECIAL THANKS

Although Jim was inherently driven toward success, that doesn't mean there weren't many people who influenced his career. For example, Gilbert Dance gave him a tremendous opportunity to grow as an entrepreneur. Not only did they partner to run the Dixie Dance gas stations together early in Jim's career, but Gilbert was also influential in his leadership style. Gilbert paved the way for Jim to leverage his tireless work ethic and infectious enthusiasm as a leader.

Jim also crossed paths with David Jones, Sr., the founder of Humana, when David was running a gas station to pay for college at the University of Louisville. At the time, Jim noticed the well-oiled machine that David ran as a third-shift employee at the station. Of course, David would go on to law school and run one of the biggest healthcare providers in the country. The two formed a mutual admiration and told many stories of their random encounters, as they became friends for life.

HIS ADVICE

Humans gravitate toward optimism. Jim Thornton was a shining example of this, as he always attracted people with a positive outlook. Although he could get angry when too much red was on the P&L, it was always a short-lived outburst. The man never held a grudge and always looked forward with hope for a brighter future; in fact, his nickname as a child was Sunny.

Jim's leadership style was unique in that he would always encourage people during the darkest times. When ventures failed, he was always there to pat someone on the back and tell them to keep working hard and continue to believe in themselves. Consequently, he was the company's biggest critic when things were going great. He never wanted anybody to rest on their laurels, thinking they couldn't get better or could afford to be complacent.

Aspiring entrepreneurs should find wisdom in Jim's sunny

disposition and unique leadership style. Jim was also known as the "get it done" type of person. *If a person came to him with an idea for a business, his advice would always be, just to do it. What's the worst thing that could happen? You can always go back to whatever it was you were doing beforehand.*

"If a person came to him with an idea for a business, his advice would always be, just to do it. What's the worst thing that could happen? You can always go back to whatever it was you were doing beforehand."

PART 2

2016 INDUCTEES: KENT OYLER, COLONEL HARLAND SANDERS, CAREY SMITH, AND ROBERT B. TRUSSELL JR.

KENT OYLER

Although I was born in Lafayette, Indiana, parts of my earlier years were spent in Missouri, Iowa, Illinois, Colorado, and of course, Kentucky. While I was a child, my father worked in a corporate capacity for a company in the livestock business. The nature of that role required him to uproot the family and move around the country regularly. So I never got too familiar with any particular area. I did eventually establish roots, as an adult, in Louisville, but that's not where my entrepreneurial journey began.

THE HIGH SCHOOL ENTREPRENEUR

My first experience in running a business happened during

high school in St. Joseph, Missouri. Through the grapevine (an early form of Twitter fifty years ago), I heard that a crew was ripping out a rail line just outside of town. My friend and I spotted an opportunity to make a few bucks with that knowledge in hand.

We rented a pickup truck, drove to where the decommissioned railroad was being uprooted, picked up the abandoned ties, and sold them by word of mouth or through an advertisement in the local newspaper. In case you're wondering what people did with old railroad ties, most found use as garden walls or fences.

Our business model wasn't sophisticated. We established railroad tie pickup routes, expanded the marketing, and I created an accounting system of sorts. And it worked. Building off that success, we expanded to other verticals; one of which was tearing down old farms for people. The scrap wood from the barn siding was sold to craft shops and used to panel basement walls. We also collected hand-hewn beams, roofing, feeders, gates, and whatever else we could salvage from old farms. People in the area could repurpose just about anything and were willing to pay a good price for our salvaged products. *Never underestimate the money-making value of a pickup truck.*

The work was hard, as we were out in the blazing hot Missouri sun for most of the day. At the end of most weeks, however, we had a thousand dollars in cash in our hands, which was extremely good money for high school kids in those days. It was certainly enough to feed my entrepreneurial spirit.

FINDING MY WAY TO LOUISVILLE

The following summer, my parents moved to Colorado, and I went off to college in Boulder. The summer after my freshman year, I restarted and expanded the business as Oyler Salvage using a new pickup and a fifth-wheel trailer. That summer, I had seven people working for me. I made about $35,000 in three months and bought the biggest stereo system you could find for my fraternity house room. Savings wasn't yet top of mind for me at nineteen years old, but I did end up having to use my earnings to pay for the rest of my college tuition when my parents divorced later that year.

My mother wound up living in Kentucky. That is how I found my way to Louisville. After I graduated, I moved in temporarily with her. I had planned to attend grad school in the fall at Southern Methodist University in Dallas. To help me pay for the tuition, I had a bank job lined up in the area. Unfortunately, fate doesn't always align with our plans for the future. Just as I was about to travel south, another Texas banking crisis hit, and my job disappeared. That left me uncertain about what to do next.

My instincts, and my mother, suggested that I stay in Kentucky, get a job at a local bank, and attend the University of Louisville for my MBA. That's exactly what I did, and the rest is history. As is often the case, the unexpected change of plans worked out quite well and set me on the path that got me to where I am today.

THE PLIGHT OF AN INTRAPRENEUR

When I finished graduate school, I worked as an officer in the treasury management department of Citizens Fidelity Bank (now PNC), which was an interesting experience because it was a new field and very intrapreneurial. I kept coming up with ideas that worked out great for the bank, but they didn't do much for my career.

Finally, one of my customers, Henry Heuser, recruited me to become the Treasurer for his company. It was a large family business, called the Henry Vogt Co., where he was promoted from Treasurer to Chief Executive Officer. I took over for him in 1982 and served the company for fifteen years, eventually rising to Chief Financial Officer. In 1985, I was named *Cashflow* magazine Treasurer of the Year.

At some point, I realized that I was a reasonably well-paid executive, but that wasn't what I *really* wanted to be. I wanted to make my own decisions and be my own boss; I wanted to be an entrepreneur. But I had a problem: I was in my mid-thirties at that point and had a wife and young family, as well as a house and plenty of other bills to pay. I didn't know how I was going to be able to support all that while starting my own business.

When I told Henry Heuser that I wanted to make a go of it on my own, he pleaded with me to stay. He told me how much he appreciated what I was doing for their company. When he realized that I felt truly compelled to become an entrepreneur, he made me a game-changing offer. He said, "Why don't you stay here and keep getting a paycheck for your work? That way, you won't have to worry about paying the bills. And how about this: anything over sixty hours, while you're here, is yours." It seemed like a reasonable compromise and gave me permission to do a little entrepreneurial fishing on the side. I wouldn't need to worry about supporting my family without a job and I could still chase my many ideas for startups.

My first solo endeavor at Vogt was another intrapreneurial effort, but this one was scalable. Vogt was in the metal manufacturing business. One of the bigger moneymakers they had was selling large commercial ice machines. I figured we could sell even more machines if we offered to lease them to customers and earn interest on the paper, and that's what I did.

I saw firsthand that the leasing business had amazing potential. I had grown it so fast inside Vogt that it was competing for capital with the machine tool budget. Leadership came to the decision that we had to sell off the leasing portfolio, which was worth around $6 million at the time. With the idea of wanting to do something on my own, I thought that maybe I could buy the portfolio.

Fortunately, I found a friendly banker who was willing to underwrite a highly leveraged buyout. He worked relentlessly to make sure I had the financing I needed and with just $2,000 down, I was able to buy the $6 million portfolio. This was the beginning of Icelease Limited Partnership and my related portfolio management company called OPM services, Inc. *If you're looking for entrepreneurial success, finding a friendly banker is almost essential.*

OPM SERVICES FLOURISHES

I still had my day job when Vogt's board decided to sell the company's four divisions. My last task there as CFO was to sell the forge, valve, heat transfer, and ice machine divisions. After selling the first three divisions, the final deal to sell the ice machine division, along with the Icelease portfolio, was ready to close when, at literally the eleventh hour, the buyer, York, hired a new CEO who decided to freeze everything. Quickly, the deal fell apart, and I was in a very difficult situation, having exhausted our credit lines. *This is where I learned that the deal is not done until the check clears the bank.*

The night after the York deal fell through, I got up at 3:00 a.m. and anxiously rethought my options. By the time I arrived at the office, I had come up with what I thought was the best solution for the company and my career moving forward, which was for my leasing company, Icelease, to buy Vogt's $20 million ice manufacturing business. Again, my friendly bankers helped out.

For several years, I operated and grew the ice business and the leasing portfolio. Together, those businesses were profitable and employed a couple of hundred people. In 2006, I wrapped up the leasing business and sold the manufacturing company to a group of investors. The business resold again to a PE firm and still operates today in Old Louisville.

In 1997, I also founded OPM Flats, which operated hundreds of heavy-duty and dimensional flat cars called free runners on railroads across North America. OPM Flats ended up being the biggest player in that niche industry until we began to challenge rail industry giant TTX. It became clear that my railroad business would no longer have much room to grow, so I sold the business to a partner who manufactured the rail cars for us, ending what was one of my better entrepreneurial runs. That business also continues to operate today under a new name.

HIGH-SPEED ENTREPRENEURIALISM

While still managing the ice and railroad endeavors, one day in 1996 I made a phone call and accidentally connected with a man named David Gibbs. I vaguely knew of him because we went to the same church. Truthfully, I don't even remember the reason for the misdirected call, but we ended up chatting about what he was doing. David told me that he was working on a new business in the *broadband* industry. I told him, "Well, that sounds interesting. You know, I do some entrepreneurial things as well. Why don't we get together for lunch and talk about some ideas?"

David agreed to meet with me. He showed up at lunch with a ragged alligator-clipped business plan. David was always a great idea man, but he knew he needed help to execute and scale. That made us a pretty good fit because those things were strengths of mine.

We ended up forming a partnership and co-founding a company. I gave David a desk in my office at OPM and a bit of money to get started. The idea was to form a revenue-sharing model with the cable TV companies. Our business, High-Speed Access Corporation (HSAC), would install the headend equipment, manage the network, and sell to the customers. Effectively, we rented the cable lines.

Timing means a lot to an entrepreneur—almost as much as having the support of a friendly banker. In this case, our timing was perfect. HSAC hit the market just as demand for broadband connections trended massively upward.

The cable companies we partnered with weren't first-tier providers, but we worked with several second-tier providers and made a lucrative business out of it. There was another company doing the same thing, called Roadrunner, but they were a Silicon Valley business with a lot of venture capital behind them. We sold mostly in suburban and exurban markets and weren't a direct competitor to them. They were already pretty big, but we were growing fast.

With David's ideas and my ability to execute and scale, the business took off. In fact, everything happened at lightning speed. I ended up with the role of President at HSAC, and soon enough, we secured venture capital, hired good people, and rented the old three-story building that Vogt Company formerly occupied, which became our network operations center.

Seemingly in the blink of an eye, we employed hundreds of people and expanded our network to Denver, Colorado. All the big cable companies were based in Denver in those days, so scaling in that market made a lot of sense. We also acquired another company with operations in the same area. Within a period of two years, we had gone from talking about some wild ideas sketched on a yellow pad during lunch to employing close to 1,000 people and having offices all over the country.

Venture capital was a big part of our success; Microsoft co-founder Paul Allen even invested money in us a few times. With the help of Chrysalis Ventures, we raised over $70 million from VCs. In 1999, with backing from JPMorgan, Bank of America, CIBC, and Lehman, we went public on the Nasdaq, and HSAC became the largest IPO in the history of the Commonwealth of Kentucky. For a period in 1999, HSAC also had the largest market cap of any Kentucky public company. We also minted twenty-five new millionaires among our employees.

The IPO experience proved extremely beneficial to HSAC, but it was exhausting for me on a personal level. I would get up Monday morning, fly to Denver, and return home to Kentucky on Friday. Rinse and repeat every week. As you can imagine, that level of intensity can become problematic for anybody. I seriously considered moving the family to Denver but decided that Kentucky was our home. That's when I learned that running a public company is a completely different animal from being a startup entrepreneur. I kept up that pace for only a short period before I decided to exit the business and hire a CEO in Denver to run the company.

No longer a restricted officer, I was finally able to secure a bit of liquidity. I leveraged $1 million of my money and $4 million from other HSAC investors to create the Metro United Way New Business Challenge, which eventually raised over $25 million for United Way. David and I also funded the public radio station renovations naming the building after our company. HSAC money also built a big park on River Road in Louisville and funded countless other civic projects. The bottom line is that a lot of good came out of the money made by investors and employees in HSAC.

Prior to the IPO, we spun out another company called Darwin Networks, which was the digital subscriber line (DSL) version of broadband. We received an offer of around $800 million from AT&T for that new company, but the venture capitalists didn't think it was enough. Unfortunately, the company never was sold and went bankrupt with the dot-com crash of 2000. Remember what I said about timing being everything?

HSAC survived the burst of the tech bubble and ended up selling to Charter Communications. Happily, we had already built our network operations center in Louisville, and there are still around 2,000 legacy jobs there today that originated with HSAC.

AFTER HSAC

I tried to retire after I exited HSAC. It turned out that I wasn't yet ready for that stage of life. So I turned OPM into an entrepreneurial support organization where we co-founded, coached, invested in, and managed dozens of other companies. Over the years, I accrued twenty co-founder titles making me the proverbial serial entrepreneur. Helping other entrepreneurs to get started, gather momentum, and make a difference in the world has always been a passion of mine.

In 2014, Greater Louisville Inc. (GLI), The Metro Chamber of Commerce found itself in trouble over a falling out with the Mayor and other issues. I was recruited off the board to become GLI's President and CEO and execute a turnaround. By 2019, we had fought back to health and were recognized as the national Chamber of the Year. It was an amazing experience to be part of such a big transformation for a civic organization I cared deeply about. As with any business endeavor, this took a lot of hard work from a lot of great people.

I didn't want to stay until my retirement age at GLI as I had a strong desire to start another business while I still had the time, so I departed in 2020, just ahead of the pandemic, handing the reins to my capable COO. I will probably forever have an entrepreneurial spirit and see innovation and business as ways to positively change the world.

By the spring of 2020, with COVID-19 raging, I was still trying to figure out if I was going to pursue a CEO role at a startup or see if I had an idea of my own for a business worth pursuing. As I was sorting that out, the Dean for the

University of Louisville's College of Business called and asked me to come to work part time for him. Since then, I've been an Entrepreneur in Residence for Employer Engagement, performing business outreach and strategy for the college. Today, I still enjoy serving in that role, as well as the CEO of OPM Services Inc.

A SPECIAL THANKS

My wife, Kathy, has always been incredibly supportive of my entrepreneurial journey. There's no question that I would not be who I am today without her. At times, she has been my business and personal advisor; other times, she has been an amazing entertainer, hosting large and small social events for colleagues and key business contacts. She has always been a tour de force in my success.

Also, I want to take another moment to thank Henry Heuser who was the boss who gave me the sixty-hour deal, which allowed me to dip my toes into the entrepreneurial waters. He remains a good friend and mentor in my business and civic life today.

David Jones Jr., Doug Cobb, and Bob Saunders were exceptional venture capitalists for HSAC. Their firm, Chrysalis Ventures, was essential to scaling the businesses that shaped my success.

And my friendly bankers, Pat Sullivan and Dennis Heishman. Thanks for believing.

Another person I owe special thanks to is David Gibbs. HSAC was his idea. Also, Chuck Woods, who was my Chief Financial Officer (CFO) and business partner at OPM.

On the civic side of my life, Alberta Allen was an incredibly special person. Her mentorship, as a philanthropist, inspired Kathy and me to become heavily involved in The United Way, which I still consider to be a great accomplishment. This year, we are chairing Metro United Way's general campaign together.

There were numerous others who have impacted my journey in an extremely positive way, too many to name here. The key takeaway is that nobody can make a significant impact on his or her own. To have an entrepreneurial spirit is the foundation to make a difference, but the people around you are instrumental in getting your mission accomplished.

MY ADVICE

Entrepreneurs take risks, produce value for investors, and create jobs that help people to become self-sufficient. To initiate that turnaround at GLI, we started with Simon Sinek's famous notion to "find your why." He advises to start by discovering why you're doing what you're doing.

At GLI, we examined Sinek's famous words as deeply as we could. We talked about why we cared about job creation and understood that it allows people to take care of themselves. When that happens, people take care of their families, they get involved with the schools, they help the community, and so on. *"Through business, you can create jobs. Through jobs, you can create sustainable people. And when someone has a job, it's the best form of philanthropy you can offer."* That was GLI's why. It is also mine. As an entrepreneur, I advise you to take Simon Sinek's words to heart and find your why. That should be your first step.

If you're in the corporate world, you likely live with some level of comfort. But that can be a trap. You might have a spouse, kids, a beautiful home, a country club membership, and all the conveniences of modern life. But you don't have to quit your job to pursue your entrepreneurial dream. After working for fifteen years in an executive role before becoming an entrepreneur, I feel compelled to tell you that there is always a way to achieve your dreams.

Many people I've spoken with, who are in such a position of complacency, feel like they have to pivot 180 degrees to chase their dreams; what they may not realize is that they can pivot 30 degrees at a time or even less. In other words, you might feel like you have to quit your day job and be willing to abandon everything you've accomplished to become an entrepreneur. I'm living proof that such a notion is false.

When I seized the opportunity presented by my boss at the time, Henry Heuser, I began my entrepreneurial journey and I kept my day job. My family, home, and all the other niceties we acquired didn't need to be thrown out. Did it kick in after sixty hours working the day job? Yes. Was it hard work? Sure. But if you have dreams and you're already successful in some capacity, I'm sure you're no stranger to hard work.

I took that first step to achieve my dream; then I took another and another until I went all-in. You can use the same approach. Give yourself permission to "fish on the side."

> "I took that first step to achieve my dream; then I took another and another until I went all-in. You can use the same approach. Give yourself permission to 'fish on the side.'"

COLONEL HARLAND SANDERS

 *This chapter is based on the personal memories and recollections of Colonel Sanders's great-granddaughter, Elizabeth Ruggles-Pitchford (granddaughter of Mildred Sanders Ruggles) and his grandson J. Trigg Adams (son of Margaret Sanders).*

In 1890, an American icon was born in Henryville, Indiana. Harland David Sanders (aka Colonel Sanders) was raised with a Christian upbringing as the oldest of three children. The family lived in a quaint four-room house and just barely made ends meet.

Harland's father, Wilbur David Sanders, died when Harland was five years old. After his passing, Harland's mother remarried a couple of times. She married her next husband in 1899 and he died only a year later. In 1902, Harland's mother married William Broaddus. Unfortunately, Harland did not have a good relationship with his mother's third husband. At the same time, he was also becoming quite disenchanted with school, citing algebra as intolerable. By 1903, he dropped out of the seventh grade.

Unhappy in his home life and unwilling to pursue his education, Harland left home initially to live and work on a nearby farm. He moved to southern Indiana to begin working in a variety of odd jobs after one year of working on the farm. It would take almost another three decades for Harland to begin to fulfill his destiny as one of the most successful entrepreneurs in the state of Kentucky and arguably, the greatest brand ambassador in the history of American business.

After several unsuccessful attempts at finding a career, including as a railway worker, a fireman on the Rock Island Line, a lawyer (being disbarred for punching out his first client for nonpayment of his successful defense), owner of his own ferry boat company, a steam paddle wheeler (until the bridge from Louisville was built), and a tire salesman, Harland finally caught a break at thirty-four years old in 1942. He was working at a manufacturing plant in New Jersey for Michelin. The plant closed, which precipitated Harland's initial move to the great commonwealth of Kentucky.

Harland relocated to Winchester, Kentucky to work as a tire salesman for Michelin. While on the job, he had a chance encounter with the general manager of Standard Oil of Kentucky. The two hit it off and the oil executive asked Harland if he would run a service station for him in Nicholasville. Harland agreed and ran the station successfully from 1924 to 1930.

SANDERS COURT AND CAFÉ

In 1930, bad timing briefly interrupted Harland's path to success when the Great Depression took its toll and forced his station to close. At this point, Harland had proved his ability to run a station and the Shell Oil Company offered him the chance to operate another station in North Corbin, Kentucky on the east side of the intersection of US 25 and 25E This is where Harland Sanders began his food service journey.

Making the most of his opportunity, Harland agreed to run the station rent-free while paying the company a percentage of his sales. Subsequently, Harland always loved to cook for people; it was his greatest passion. With that in mind, he decided to cook for his customers, offering country ham, steaks, and (of course) chicken. If there were no customers for food, his family consumed it; if sold, he would cook for the family later.

Southern hospitality also played a role in Sanders's

approach to business. He didn't want to provide ordinary food or service. Rather, he wanted to perfect his recipes and make people comfortable. Soon enough, he opened a full-service restaurant and built the first motel in the southeast across the street from that gas station. The restaurant/motel was called Sanders Court and Café.

Many people traveling north or south on the old rural route US 25 ate and stayed at Sanders Court and Café because it was comfortable and the food was good. That location would go through many incarnations and eventually become the site of a museum in 1990.

Sanders Court and Café became a popular place. There, he started experimenting with chicken recipes and cooking methods in order to obtain a consistently good quality. People loved the chicken, which Harland took special pride in preparing. They also appreciated the place to stay. Perhaps more than anything, they enjoyed the service and hospitality provided by Harland. They appreciated it so much that word soon got out about the appeal of the establishment. Word got out because he pioneered the strategy of offering to paint roadside barns in return for the right to advertise his business, up to a hundred miles in both directions!

With Harland gaining popularity in the eyes of the local citizens and tourists, Governor Ruby Lafoon commissioned him to become a Kentucky Colonel in 1935. The title held no military rank; rather, it was an honorary moniker given to him mostly because he had become an extremely popular local public figure due to his continual giving of any extra money he didn't need to various charities and orphanages. Thus began the legacy of Colonel Sanders, aka The Colonel.

OVERCOMING ADVERSITY

Colonel Sanders encountered his fair share of challenges during his entrepreneurial journey. That popular gas station/motel partly burned down in 1939. Undeterred, Sanders rebuilt and enlarged the motel and expanded the restaurant to 140 seats. This was where he perfected his recipe for frying chicken in a pressure fryer. The "Original Recipe" for Kentucky Fried Chicken was finalized at this point, so he copyrighted the name and image. He also received a patent on his modification of the pressure cookers that were necessary for the nongreasy preparation of the chicken. The spices are kept secret to this day.

With perfection attained, The Colonel franchised his secret recipe to a restaurant in Louisville and later to an operator of a restaurant in south Salt Lake, Utah named Pete Harman. The addition to the menu proved an unthinkable success. Not only was the chicken itself a hit, but the product added a spirit of southern hospitality to an establishment where the concept was unprecedented. No other restaurant in the area featured a menu item so distinctly southern and so remarkably appealing in a comfort food sort of way. From there, several other restaurant owners sought to franchise The Colonel's recipe and instilled it in their menus with similarly outstanding success. The one-page franchise agreement stipulated a royalty to him of five cents per chicken (three dinners per chicken, which had to be cut to his specifications), as well as the size and quality of the chickens. He retained ownership of the modified pressure cookers. If a franchisee didn't measure up to his standards, he would revoke the franchise rights and retrieve the cookers, per the agreement.

Unfortunately, The Colonel's own restaurant didn't fare as well as the recipe. The project to build the interstate highway system included I-75, which significantly reduced traffic on US 25, where Sanders's restaurant was located. People didn't need to travel the same backroad at a slower pace. Instead, they got on the highway and took a more direct and much faster route to most of their destinations. At age sixty-five, The Colonel was forced to sell the eatery. Sanders Court and Café was no longer in existence.

In 1959, Sanders opened a new restaurant in Shelbyville, Kentucky. While owning and operating that new establishment, he also traveled to other restaurants, using his daughter Margaret's 1950 Dodge. When he arrived, he offered to make his chicken for the restaurant and negotiated franchise rights for the recipe (the same one-page agreement).

After word spread about the success of his chicken to an even greater extent than what happened in Utah, Sanders was finally able to stop traveling, as restaurant owners began to come to him from all over the United States and even a little beyond. Soon enough, franchising rights were sold internationally to the United Kingdom. Meanwhile, Sanders had begun building locations in Canada, of which he retained total ownership and operations, and established a charitable trust.

THE FACE OF THE FRANCHISE

Due to The Colonel's perseverance, his "finger lickin' good chicken" became popular beyond Kentucky and throughout most of North America. From 1959 to 1963, KFC expanded to over 600 locations, which became a bit much for a seventy-three-year-old Harland Sanders to handle.

Colonel Sanders sold the Kentucky Fried Chicken Corporation for $2 million (equivalent to around $17 million in 2022) in 1964 to Jack C. Massey and the future governor of Kentucky and fellow Kentucky Entrepreneur Hall of Fame member John Y. Brown. Former Governor Brown was the son of his good friend and lawyer, John Y. Brown Sr., who had drawn up the franchise agreement. With that contract,

The Colonel was also given a lifetime salary to become the face of the franchise, which is something he excelled at.

In 1965, The Colonel moved to Mississauga, Ontario, which is a suburb of Toronto. The goal was to oversee the progress and quality of his Canadian franchises, which he still owned at that time. In fact, the property he bought there remained his home until the time of his death in 1980.

Colonel Sanders remained the brand ambassador for KFC for many years, traveling throughout the United States and Canada. He also stayed active in overseeing the quality of the company's food. He would even walk into the kitchen of some franchises unannounced and perform spot checks. If he found something about the food quality not to his liking, he would show the workers how to do things properly. Occasionally, his temper got the best of him and he might let out a few choice words while sliding a few plates onto the ground in the process. After selling the franchise, the new owners had to make some cutbacks in the quality of the ingredients to certain items to optimize profits. This didn't sit well with Sanders.

The Colonel was particularly outspoken about the gravy and the audacity of the new ownership to create an extra crispy version of his chicken. He repeatedly referred to the gravy as slop or wallpaper paste. In an edition of the *Louisville Courier-Journal*, he also called the extra crispy menu item a "damn fried dough ball stuck to a piece of chicken." One can't help but wonder what he would think of some of the more recent menu selections.

THE COLONEL, THE GIVER

Although The Colonel had a fiery personality when it came to what he saw as diminishing the quality of his food, he had a heart of gold, especially for children or anyone in need of assistance. He made a lot of money from selling his franchise and by serving as its brand ambassador for many years. Interestingly enough, he kept almost none of his cash windfall. Just before his passing, KFC Corp did research showing that he had given over $20 million to charities over the years!

In his last few years on earth, he founded the Colonel Harland Sanders Charitable Organization, which remains a registered Canadian charity today, and has made many substantial donations to children's hospitals in Canada and the United States. It was taken into their own private hands by the men he had installed as trustees. In particular, he gave most of his money, at the time of his death, to the March of Dimes, St. Jude's Children's Research Hospital in Memphis, Tennessee, and the many Shriners Hospitals located in the United States, Canada, and Mexico. The Salvation Army was also one of his favorite organizations to donate to.

There was always a special place in The Colonel's heart for children, and he left that altruistic notion of love with his charitable donations as a wonderfully admirable aspect of his legacy.

A SPECIAL THANKS

Sanders remained a man of faith throughout his life, citing God as the biggest source of his inspiration and motivation. He and his wife, Claudia, were baptized in the Jordan River in 1970. Also noteworthy when exploring his religious beliefs were his good friendships with Billy Graham and Jerry Falwell, who also benefited from his largesse.

For every victory in Sanders's life, there seemed to be another obstacle. With strong faith by his side, however, he found a way to walk with God and overcome anything that stood in his way of fulfilling his destiny as an entrepreneur and a philanthropist.

The Colonel was also a strong family man and extremely grateful for the opportunity to spend time with his grandchildren. Often, he took them out for his surprise visits to local KFC franchises and for public appearances, where he would dress in his iconic outfit, sign autographs, and talk to just about anybody who wanted to engage him about his story or the chicken that made him famous. Colonel Sanders was truly an American icon and will forever be etched in the minds of Kentucky entrepreneurs.

HIS ADVICE

In June 1980, Harland David Sanders was diagnosed with acute leukemia and died of pneumonia at a Louisville hospital about six months later. He was ninety years old. Although it took The Colonel many years to attain his pinnacle of success, his story is one of a rich and flavorful (pardon the pun) life. At the time of his death, the KFC franchise had expanded to over 6,000 outlets worldwide.

Today, there are over 22,000 KFC locations spread over 135 countries. The brand has a current valuation of around $8.3 billion and is part of the parent corporation called YUM! Not bad for a boy from a small, rural town who dropped out of seventh grade. Even today, his face is the most recognized visage in the world, but in the late summer of 1980, he stated that his proudest achievement was his charitable work.

Those who knew him best would say that perseverance would be his best advice to any aspiring entrepreneur. Perhaps nobody embodied that lesson more than Harland David Sanders. Even after a fire and the interstate highway system destroyed his restaurant on two separate occasions,

The Colonel persevered and reached a level of success to be admired by anyone. The following quote says it all:

"I've only had two rules. Do all you can and do it the best you can. It's the only way you ever get that feeling of accomplishing something."

"I've only had two rules. Do all you can and do it the best you can. It's the only way you ever get that feeling of accomplishing something."

CLOSING THOUGHTS FROM J. TRIGG ADAMS

My contributions to this chapter come from the experiences of spending my earliest years growing up as one grandson who lived at Sanders Court, worked the cash register at the restaurant, pumped gas, and rented rooms. Later, I washed dishes at Harman's Café in Salt Lake, cooked chicken at many franchise locations, and oversaw quality control for the state of Florida. I still stand in awe of the man who most people don't really know.

CAREY SMITH

I started my own business not because I wanted to change the world or get rich (definitely not) but for the same reason many people do: to be my own boss. I thought I could do things better than the next guy and had gotten to the point where I didn't want to work another day for somebody else.

It was not a spur-of-the-moment decision. I'd been thinking about it for years. My whole working life, I had observed how businesses were run and mentally filed away examples of what companies did right and wrong. I was particularly tuned to the way managers treated employees, for better or for worse (especially for worse). Although I was lucky to have had some good bosses, I was motivated even more by the bad ones. I told myself, "If I ever have a business, I'm not going to act like them."

I have had a lot of bosses, having worked since childhood, and I'm sure those childhood experiences predisposed me to later strike out on my own; they even played a role in the kind of business I went into. When I was a kid, we moved all the time. We could have easily been mistaken for a family on the lam. My old man wasn't running from the law, though; he simply changed jobs at the drop of a hat in search of incrementally higher pay. Consequently, our family of six (I was the oldest of four kids) never lived in any town long enough to feel connected to it. I probably went to nine or ten schools by the time I graduated high school.

If this had any benefit, it was that it made us self-reliant and toughened us up. I know it set me on a lifelong path of being a contrarian. I never tried to be part of any group and never looked for affirmation from my peers. Over time, I came to assume I could do everything on my own.

As the oldest of my brothers and sisters, I was in charge of making sure the chores got done. Figuring out how to wheedle and bribe my siblings (today, it's called incentivizing) was my first experience in management. Because everywhere we moved, from Alabama to Missouri to Arkansas, seemed to have summers hotter than the place before and nowhere had air-conditioning, one of the chores was cooling off the house. We would go outside, turn on the hose, spray the roof, and watch as an impressive mist rose off the hot shingles. Our primitive attempts at "evaporative cooling" later inspired my first company.

Our family was never what you'd call flush with the ready, so I was always looking for ways to contribute to the family coffers and put some change in my pocket. At eight, I sold crafts and Christmas cards door to door before upgrading to a newspaper delivery route. By high school, I was washing uniforms with scalding steam cleaners and working as a janitor for the local newspaper in a rickety old wooden building full of chain-smoking reporters. (The way they carelessly discarded cigarettes—I was always relieved not to find the building a smoldering ruin when I reported for duty.)

All this "worldly experience" made me confident and, I'm sure, a bit cocky. About midway through my senior year, I was audacious enough to think I could do a better job running the school than the people in charge.

Somehow, I convinced the principal and school district superintendent to try it. This was in 1970, and they were probably just grateful I wasn't advocating a sit-in. They agreed to let me and a few other classmates take over the school for three days by creating the courses and arranging the schedules. My team of six fellow students surveyed our classmates to learn the subjects they were interested in and what their parents, friends, teachers, and assorted others could possibly teach. (At this time, we were living in northern Virginia, where government employees, politicians, and scientists were a dime a dozen.) Eventually, we scheduled 252 classes over three days for 1,000 kids.

The experience convinced me that I might *really* be able to do something, or better yet, run something when the day came. It took a dozen years before I figured it out.

THE IMPORTANCE OF FAILING FAST

By then, I was underwriting reinsurance out of Dallas, which is insurance that insurance companies buy to insure themselves against big claims.

I specialized in oil and gas industries and spent time in hot, dusty oil fields. But what stuck with me most about those years was when a company's vice president told me and a few others, without hesitation, "You know, I could afford to pay you all twice as much, but why should I, when you'll work for less?" I didn't quit on the spot, but that statement came to symbolize for me everything that was wrong with the way businesses were run. I was sure I could do better. As soon as I had a plan in place, I traded an 8:00 a.m. to 5:00 p.m. job for one that consumed me 24/7 and considered it a good trade.

Any true entrepreneur is always looking for a new or different path, always thinking about what could work and what might sell. My first business, which I started with my father, manufactured and sold roof sprinklers to cool industrial buildings, an idea that came from that childhood experience. It became a pursuit of failure. That's how I describe it now, at least. I was fixated on the product, the next sale, and the next installation. I was convinced that my persistence would eventually pay off and that the product I was peddling would one day be installed on factory and warehouse roofs across the South and everywhere else summer heat turns large workplaces, for which air-conditioning is not realistic, into sweatshops.

Did the product work? Yes. But it was always a hard sell. The technology was difficult for the public to understand. I spent a lot of time explaining thermodynamics, physiology, the latent heat of water, and so on. Did the business grow at all? Yes, but never enough to add more people to the payroll and lighten my load. I grew exhausted. Every installation involved physical labor, and the traveling was draining too. I was also losing confidence in the product. It was entirely outside the building, while the people it was designed to help were inside. Seriously, what business owner wants somebody climbing all over their roof? If I didn't entirely understand that then, I do now.

Eventually, I understood that the roof sprinkler would never be my ticket over the rainbow. I began looking around for other opportunities, eventually finding one in a trade magazine. I saw a small ad for a large-diameter industrial ceiling fan. "Holy cow," I thought. (The fan was originally designed to cool dairy barns.) I instantly recognized the fan's potential and cut out the ad. Then, like a doofus, I lost it. Luckily, it ran again, or I might not be writing this today. It was only a matter of days before I was flying out to California to visit the small machine shop where the fan was made. I felt like I was flying on a magic carpet; I knew at last I was onto something big. After twelve years of pushing roof sprinklers, I was able to sell my part of the company to my old man and use the money to go into the fan business.

Today, when I meet entrepreneurs who remind me of myself, the ones who are fixated on their product, not the ones whose only fixation is a big payoff at exit, I try to get them to see beyond their nose. I want them to take a step back and be honest with themselves. Consider the possibility that there might just be a better solution to the problem they're trying to solve if they give themselves the chance to see it. In other words, don't be so reluctant to acknowledge failure that you prolong the experience and delay the inevitable. After all, as any motivational speaker will tell you, it's only failure if you let it be.

A COOL COW IS A COMFORTABLE COW

When I first visited the machine shop, they had built seventeen fans. But the guys were machinists and engineers; they had no experience with sales or marketing. So I told them I would sell the fans. But I needed exclusivity, and I included in the contract that if we were successful at selling the fans, we would have the opportunity to buy the patents.

There were six of us early on, marketing the never-before-seen products to a skeptical audience, struggling to show them at trade shows like Modex in Chicago, where, as you might imagine, it was damn near impossible to display a twenty-four-foot diameter ceiling fan. But slowly, the fans began developing a fanbase of their own, as people tried them and could immediately feel the difference. The first year, we sold 146 fans; in the second year, 420. Funny how you remember things like that. Maybe it tells you how caught up in the excitement we were. To me, that's what being an entrepreneur is all about.

As demand increased, the machine shop had a hard time keeping up. Finally, some problems with components led to a recall of hundreds of fans, which led us to decide that it was time to part ways. So I bought the IP and we began manufacturing the fans ourselves at a machine shop in Lexington, Kentucky.

BECOMING CHIEF BIG ASS

At that time, we called ourselves The HVLS Fan Company, because that was the product we made and sold: high-volume low-speed fans. We thought it was straightforward and descriptive, but it didn't exactly roll off the tongue. At the same time, whenever we answered the phone, we would hear, "Are you the guys who make those big-ass fans?" "Sir, yes, sir." We might have been slow, but we weren't total dummies. We started using the term "big ass" to describe our fans in advertising, and in 2002 we officially changed the company's name.

Of course, if we were going to be Big Ass Fans, we needed a mascot, and we already knew what its name would be: Fanny. We heard about a donkey in a field a few miles away and scurried out there one afternoon, waiting on the other side of the fence to snap the ideal image from the rear of the donkey looking back at us. The image became our logo and Fanny became our mascot.

Not only did we have a name that connected with our target audience; it also rankled some members of the public, especially the 5 percent who are just dying to be upset about something. When a postmaster in Louisville refused to deliver our marketing postcards, we turned it to our advantage by alerting the media. For a while, the Lexington airport refused to allow us to display advertising due to the objections of one overly cantankerous board member. Now a Big Ass Fan keeps travelers cool as they wait to go through security. People picketed across the street when we painted our name and logo on the side of our building. And people loved to call and swear at us about our ungodly name, which we had fun with in our marketing. We always, coyly but rightfully, took the high road by pointing out the number of times the word *ass* appeared in the Bible (forty-six).

Occasionally, we'd be told by some cracker-jack consultants that we needed to change our name, but our customers loved it. For us, it had the added advantage of personifying our guiding principle: We listened to our customers and they gave us our name.

At the same time, we knew with a name like that, we would just be a joke if we didn't totally wow people with the quality of our products and service, so that's what we did. We never cut corners and we constantly improved. We used only the best components. We were always available to talk to customers and answer questions. If there were problems, we made sure we solved them to the customer's satisfaction, no matter how much it cost us, and there were a few times that it cost us plenty. I still believe that's the only way to do business.

FROM FARMS TO HOMES

For the almost twenty years I ran the company, the story

of Big Ass Fans was one of constant expansion. If you'd asked me in the early 2000s how big I thought the market for the fans was, I might have said 50,000. But within a decade, we were manufacturing and shipping out 100,000 per year. Early on, because of all my contacts from the roof sprinkler business, our market had gone from strictly agricultural to industrial workplaces: warehouses, factories, and anywhere that was too big to install air-conditioning economically. From there, the fans moved into sports facilities and stadiums.

When we bought a 98,000-square-foot facility, I remember thinking we had hit the big time. "No way will we ever fill this place up," I said. But within a few years, we had outgrown it and were hiring like crazy. We built a new headquarters and a new 44,000-square-foot R&D lab shaped like an airplane hangar.

We realized we needed to design a quieter, less industrial fan when people started installing them in places that didn't fit. We learned a lesson when a historic church in Brooklyn, New York installed an industrial fan, and the congregation could hear its hum during prayers. They were unhappy, but we were determined to make things right. So we implored them to let us somehow make it up to them. We'd do anything, we assured them. "Anything? Well, the church could really use some new windows," the pastor said. So $7,000 later, they had them. They were happy, and we were happy, because you only learn from your mistakes when you pay for them, and boy, did we pay for that one. We instantly got to work designing beautiful fans with completely silent motors that were soon appearing in concert halls, restaurants, and yes, churches. Lots and lots of churches. Not long after that, with the help of a New Zealand engineer living in Malaysia, we reinvented the home ceiling fan with our Haiku line, which grew rapidly to a $60 million line whose sleek looks made them an instant favorite of interior designers.

DON'T BE IN BUSINESS TO MAKE MONEY

The most important thing throughout the time I was Chief Big Ass was not our products but our people: our customers, employees, and suppliers. I wanted to go into business not because I wanted to make fans but because I wanted to run a better company than any I had worked for, one that wasn't focused on profits but people. This is why we were successful. Although we gradually gained more competitors as the concept of giant overhead fans caught on, when I sold the company almost twenty years after starting it, we still owned the market.

Much of the interest in the company's story—besides its name—can be attributed to how we did business. Contrarian to the core, we didn't operate the way most companies did. We were openly critical of them. We refused to outsource and never put profits first. We manufactured in America, used nearby suppliers so that we could keep an eye on quality, and we avoided distributors by selling direct. Of course, we needed (and wanted) to be profitable, but the most important thing to me was to build a great company that made great products and was a great place to work. Plenty of places pay lip service to the *golden rule*, but we were adamant about making sure we treated customers, employees, and suppliers as we would want to be treated.

We prided ourselves on adhering to the *golden rule* and believed in its ethical superiority, but that would be misleading. We didn't treat customers, employees, and suppliers as we liked to be treated because we were nice people; we did it because we were good capitalists. That was always my goal. Being good capitalists was why we paid more than 30 percent above the national average, provided good bonuses and benefits, and ensured that employees had the perks they wanted. That's why we didn't try to nickel and dime our suppliers into the ground (and paid them quickly). It's also why we reached out to every customer to ensure they were satisfied.

When I talk about good capitalists, I'm not talking about Certified B Corporations. Being a good capitalist does not require membership in anything or a logo flaunting your holier than thou-ness. Who are they kidding? We all know those are primarily designed to lure customers. No, good capitalists assume certain responsibilities toward society and want to make it better. They make quality products and don't build in obsolescence. Good capitalists want to see everyone rowing in the same direction with nobody confined to the galley, and they don't put profits before people.

At Big Ass Fans, we saw the relationship between profits and people as one of mutualism. We were not in business to make money but rather, to grow our business, because only by growing could we share the money we made with greater numbers of employees and ultimately the community at large. If you're in business only for the money, you lose so much.

Being in business is also a lot of fun. We had a great time seeing how the public responded to our name and donkey logo. One of my proudest moments in business was in 2003 when a city councilman in Lexington objected to our prominent mural displayed where thousands of motorists passed it each day. The councilman, who also was the same gentleman barring us from advertising at the airport, called it "uncouth behavior and not desirable in a civilized society." But it was just the backside of a donkey—an animal that brought Mary to Jerusalem and helped build civilization across the globe.

But the best time I ever had was when I sold the company for the price I wanted and made instant millionaires of people who'd worked every bit as hard as me to make the business a success.

One pearl of so-called wisdom that everyone has heard is the advice, "Do something you love, and you'll never work a day in your life." I hate that. First of all, most people don't have that option. Even worse, it implies there's something less than desirable about working. The truth is, if your only goal is to do something you love, you're probably taking the easy path.

If I had followed that advice, I probably would have majored in history in college. I love it, and because I do, it seems easy. Instead, I majored in economics, partly because the "dismal science" can be so damn challenging to understand. Decades later, I haven't lost the desire for that same kind of challenge.

AN UNORTHODOX EXIT

For nearly twenty years, I took great pride in Big Ass Fans, but even before the papers were signed on the sale, I had a good idea of my new purpose. Its origins actually came from a group of engineers (glorified tinkerers, really) within the company who experimented on projects far outside our core focus—from reducing food waste to studying insect behavior.

I love the day-to-day challenge of solving problems, and

the company's incredible annual growth (which was more than 40 percent on average over two decades) gave us the freedom to explore other potentially lucrative ideas. Even though most of the projects ultimately didn't pan out, the group's activities made coming to work each day all the more exciting.

When I parted with Big Ass Fans, I talked some of those tinkerers into coming with me, and we headed south to Austin, Texas. Here, where entrepreneurs are nearly as thick as the city's famous bats, we started a company, Unorthodox Ventures, with the goal of helping founders solve the day-to-day challenges of building businesses and brands that last.

It didn't take long to realize that most founders we met didn't have a clue about any of the basics that are essential for success. Through no fault of their own, they were living in a fantasy world, believing they had winning products that only needed an infusion of cash, a contract manufacturer, and a few carefully curated influencers to bring in the big bucks. They had been led down a primrose path to certain failure by so-called mentors, inexperienced academics, and predatory lenders in the form of greedy venture capitalists—none of whom had given them anything but platitudes.

We quickly understood that the biggest challenge of our job would be bringing them back to reality. Since what we have to offer is decades of business and manufacturing experience and what we love most is solving problems, we would do what we could to correct the misinformation that entrepreneurs had been fed and set them on a road that's less traveled but far more likely to take them somewhere they want to be.

FURTHER READING

If you're looking for the best damn business book, look no further than *Yertle the Turtle* by Dr. Seuss. You don't need to read Carnegie or Covey, Collins or Pink to know that it's not good business to treat employees, aka other people, as if they exist only to do your bidding. It's the one rule that's golden, and ignoring it is what gets Yertle in trouble. There he was, king of a "nice little pond" full of happy turtles, until one day he decides his empire isn't big enough. He orders his turtles to climb on top of each other, then sits on top of his turtle throne and claims dominion over everything he sees. This creates all kinds of hardship for a "plain little turtle" at the bottom named Mack, who speaks for his fellow turtles: "Up on top, you are seeing great sights, but down here at the bottom we, too, should have rights."

Does Yertle care about them? Of course not! But then Mack opens his mouth one more time, and his plain little burp is enough to shake the tower and send all the turtles, including Yertle, tumbling down. The lesson is clear to any six-year-old: Ignore the well-being of those who work for you, and you could find yourself waist deep in mud.

Most business books have one point to make and make it over and over. These stories also have one point to make but say it once, and we get it. My point? *Do business the right way. Don't cheap out on quality or service; abide by the golden rule, and you'll surely reap the benefits.* I hope you got it.

Now get to work!

> "Do business the right way. Don't cheap out on quality or service; abide by the *golden rule*, and you'll surely reap the benefits."

ROBERT B. TRUSSELL JR.

I grew up as the oldest of seven kids in a traditional Catholic family in Milwaukee, Wisconsin. After graduating high school, I attended Marquette University and received my bachelor's degree in business with a concentration in finance.

Like many kids of that era, I had a newspaper route when I was about eleven years old. One route wasn't enough for me, though. When other kids quit their routes, I bought them for about fifty bucks each. A savvy entrepreneur at age eleven? Probably not, but I was never one to turn down opportunities.

Delivering newspapers for three or four routes became a lot

for a kid on a bicycle to handle while going to school, doing homework (only when absolutely necessary), and whatever other activities in which I was enrolled. So I had to develop a strategy to get it all done in the most efficient way possible.

My parents were supportive of my desire to earn my own money at an early age, so Mom picked up the papers for me and strategically dropped off a bunch of them at certain parts of the neighborhood. This lightened my load for each route and allowed me to optimize my time management. It proved to be a great system most of the time.

One day, my mom didn't place a stack of newspapers with a rock securely enough. The papers blew all over the neighborhood, which created a mess. That was fine, though, because it helped me to realize a vital entrepreneurial lesson at a young age—I knew how important it would be to learn from my mistakes.

ENTREPRENEURIALISM IN MY BLOOD

I come from a long line of inventors. Fun fact: My paternal grandfather invented the spiral notebook in the early 1900s. Several decades later, our family name was still printed on at least one version of them. While attending college at Marquette, I bought a notebook in the student store and was amused to find "A genuine Trussell" printed on the inside cover.

History dictates that my grandfather ended up selling his invention to a company for a modest sum. Today, it would probably be considered little more than spare change, but I'm told the profit he received was more than fair for its time.

Although entrepreneurialism is in my blood, I've understood that not everybody is cut out for it. You have to be willing to take risks. Understanding risk and knowing how to deal with it has always been a strength of mine, which is probably why I fell in love with horse racing so easily.

HORSING AROUND

I didn't start looking for jobs in finance or anything that aligned with the degree after graduating from Marquette. Instead, with my love for horse racing in full bloom, I followed my passion and went to work at a racetrack in New York. The job didn't pay a lot, but I had a good sense for betting on the right horses, so I supported myself mostly by placing smart bets on the afternoon races. I wasn't doing anything that was going to make me wealthy, but I was winning enough to make ends meet and I learned a lot about horses.

Soon enough, I moved to Chicago, where I trained horses for three years. This wasn't a horrible job, but the horses I was training were limited (to put it nicely) in their abilities to compete. That job didn't last long anyway, as the race-track where I worked, Hawthorn, burned down in 1978 and I had to find work somewhere else. That's how I found my way to the great state of Kentucky in the early 1980s.

That tragic event had a silver lining for me, as moving to Kentucky proved to be a big break. I got a job working for a man named John Gaines at Gainesway Farm in Lexington, which was a substantial improvement from what I was doing in Chicago. No longer was I just a struggling trainer with three slow horses. I worked with an equine lawyer named Jim Philpott, selling stallion shares and rights to breed. This was the upper echelon of the horse industry. I also managed our racehorses, but this time, the horses were actually quite good. We bought Derby favorites and had a few horses trying to win championships in Europe.

After enjoying success at Gainesway, Jim and I left in the late 1980s to do our own thing. We developed a stallion season arbitrage business named Live Foal Co. with horseman Johnny Jones. But in 1991, the entire horse racing industry crumbled (it absolutely imploded). Our business became completely irrelevant and quickly went bankrupt, forcing me to find something else to do...once again.

DESPERATE TIMES

When Live Foal Co. went out of business, I was about forty

years old and had more experience with horses than I did with people. In other words, I was unhirable. Sure, I had a degree in finance, but it was a million years prior and getting a job at a bank or investment company seemed virtually impossible. So there was only one thing left for me to do—I would have to make it on my own. I had to do something entrepreneurial.

My first venture was a handicap service called Bloodline Bob. I called my picks into a computer located in Miami, and bettors could take my advice for a fee of around $25 per call. The service was advertised in the racing form, which brought in a decent amount of customers. Bloodline Bob did fairly well for a while, but I still wasn't making enough money.

At the time, I had two mortgages to pay. My wife, Martha, and I were using credit cards to buy groceries and approaching the limits on those. I needed a break; it didn't need to be in the horse business, but I needed to find a way to make more money.

There appeared to be no answers, and with nowhere else to turn, I started going to church every day to pray. I had regained my faith several years before this implosion. And one fateful day, my prayers were answered when I ran into somebody who helped me get going in the right direction.

Fortunately, I developed a lot of contacts in the horse racing business. One of them was a French horse trainer named Alain. He knew a Swedish chiropractor, named C. G., who sold a high-tech machine to clean horse stalls. He asked Alain if he would sell it for him in France. Alain, being the thoughtful guy he was, told him, "I'll do you one better. Not only will I sell it in France, but I also know someone who will sell it in the States." The guy in the states, of course, was me.

Desperate to generate any sort of income, I got on a plane to Sweden and met the guy who owned the machine that made the horse stall cleaner. We got a deal done for me to sell his product in America. Unfortunately, he didn't speak one word of English, so every time we spoke, a translator had to be involved. In fact, when we spoke over the phone, we had to use a foreign-language operator, which cost around $300 at the time. He would also send me faxes in Swedish, which I had to take to the University of Kentucky to get translated.

Another problem was that competition existed that did something similar for about one-tenth the cost. The product I was selling cost $499 and other brands were selling for around $49. That's a big problem! Of course, those products weren't nearly as good, but for one-tenth the cost, most people were willing to sacrifice some level of performance.

Between the big disparity in price and language, trying to

sell this high-tech horse stall cleaner was getting frustrating. I began to feel like it was time for me to quit and try something else. Just as I was about to follow through on that, C. G. told me about another product. He told me that a guy named Mikael Magnusson in Sweden claimed he had made the world's greatest mattress—something called a Tempur-Pedic.

SECURING EXCLUSIVITY

Despite my initial reservations, I agreed to fly to Sweden again to meet Magnusson. Turned out that he was also in the horse business, so we hit it off right away. I stayed at his home and slept on the mattress that he claimed was a game changer. I spent two or three days there, and after trying the product myself, I agreed that the mattress was better than anything else in the industry. On the last day, I told him that I was interested in selling his product in the United States. He told me to go home and write a marketing plan. He had nobody to sell it in America yet, so he would look over my plan and make his decision.

I wrote what was probably the worst marketing plan in the history of business. My idea was to sell them at truck stops because the mattress was only three inches thick, which made it extremely portable. It could easily be shoved into the back of a truck for a driver to catch a good night's sleep without having to rent a room anywhere.

For some strange reason, Magnusson liked the idea. He gave me exclusive distribution rights to sell the Tempur-Pedic mattress in the United States. The only caveat to the deal was that I had to sell 10,000 of them in a year to retain the exclusivity. Of course, that was his way to get out of the deal if we missed the targets.

Another condition of the deal was that I would need to raise my own money; Magnusson wouldn't finance me, so I raised about $500,000 from friends and family, which was an impressive feat on its own. I had to go back to all the people who lost money in my old racing partnerships and convince them to back me on this mattress deal. The irony is that they lost money in an industry I knew a lot about. In fact, I was a verifiable expert in the field. This time, I was asking them to invest more money in an industry I knew *nothing* about.

Although Mikael would not directly finance me, he did help me secure my investors. He flew in from Sweden and agreed to chat with some of them in the States. One of my biggest potential investors was my Uncle Bill in Chicago. When Mikael and I sat down at Uncle Bill's house, we showed him the product and he wrote a check for $50,000 as an investment.

I was incredibly grateful for Uncle Bill's faith and trust in me. After leaving his house, I drove Mikael back to O'Hare airport. On my way home to Lexington, I stopped at a fast-food place for a quick bite to eat. The next day, my phone rang. It was Uncle Bill. He said, "Hey, Rob, I just got off the phone with a young lady named Cindy who works at a Burger King in Lebanon, Indiana. She claims to have found a check written to you for $50,000 on the floor."

Frantically, I started going through my pockets. Of course, my uncle called me early in the morning, so I wasn't entirely conscious yet. It was probably the most embarrassing moment of my life. After a few frightening seconds of humiliation, my Uncle Bill took me off the hook and said, "How about I just write you another check and overnight it? I'll cancel that other one." That was an incredibly gracious way for my Uncle Bill to handle that situation. He had all the right in the world to blast me, but he didn't. He took the high road and gave me a second chance. Happily, I was able to reward him for that response.

Sidenote: Somewhere out there is a former Burger King worker named Cindy, who has probably told the story many times about how she once found a check for $50,000 on the floor at work, with no idea of what it amounted to. My Uncle Bill ended up sending twenty-eight grandchildren to college with his return on investment from that money.

Of course, that money was part of the initial investment that began the Tempur-Pedic distribution network in the

United States. As rocky of a beginning as the Burger King fiasco was, it actually got worse before it got better.

My idea to put the mattresses in the backs of trucks wasn't a viable business plan. I didn't realize that most of the drivers don't own the trucks and weren't willing to make long-term improvements to them. Sure, the mattress was portable enough to take from one truck to another, but most of the drivers didn't want to do that.

As it turns out, by selling to truck drivers we fell exactly 10,000 mattresses short of the 10,000 mattress requirement from my original deal with Mikael Magnusson. In other words, our total sales in this area were zero. That wasn't a problem, however, because I had other ideas to maintain that crucial distribution exclusivity in the United States and actually make money.

"BACK" IN BUSINESS

Realizing the truck driver idea wasn't going to work, we brought the mattress to chiropractors around the Milwaukee area. Unfortunately, that idea started with about as much merit as the truck stop stroke of genius. We had about five local chiropractors who had them in their offices. That's five more than the truck stop idea but still not nearly enough. We were running out of money fast.

The chiropractors, however, gave us great feedback. They told us we should make a pillow out of the same material. Most of them weren't willing to display a full-size mattress in their office, but the pillow would be a lot more manageable. I thought that might work, so I asked my manufacturers in Denmark if they could start making pillows. We helped with the shape and design specs, and they sent us a container of pillows by July 1992.

I soon discovered that there were over 40,000 practicing chiropractors in the United States. Finally, something clicked. I thought, "How do I get the word out to all of these people about the Tempur-Pedic pillow? How can I get them to at least try it and see how much better it is than anything else that's on the market? If this works, how could I scale the business into other areas?"

We thought the pillows would sell, but we didn't have a team of sales reps across the country. I mailed pillows to 500 chiropractors. Each pillow arrived in a box with a letter saying something like, "Enjoy this Tempur-Pedic Swedish neck pillow, the greatest pillow in the world." Some marketing content followed, and the note closed with an offer: "If you agree that it's the best pillow you've ever used, keep it for free with the purchase of four more. If you don't like it, we will come to pick it up at our expense. Thank you!"

Half of the recipients told us to come pick up the pillow and another quarter of them liked it enough to not give it back but also didn't buy the four more that were required to keep it. That left us with about 125 pillows successfully sold for free with the purchase of four more pillows. The long-term result was that the 125 or so chiropractors who liked it continued to buy them at a pace of around one pillow per week for their practice.

One canceled $50,000 check and a failed truck stop marketing experiment later, we finally had a sustainable business model. In the first year, we did about $300,000 in sales, and that is what got the company rolling in the right direction.

GETTING INTO RETAIL

We had kick-started our success with the chiropractors, but if we were going to scale, we knew we needed to find our way into the retail space.

The first store we thought of was Sharper Image. Our product seemed to align perfectly with their brand image; all I needed to do was convince them. I called the purchasing people at Sharper Image about 10,000 times and they never returned my calls. Then my wife, Martha, and I went out shopping for Christmas gifts at a mall in Cincinnati, Ohio. We walked by Brookstone and Martha said, "Hey, go get that pillow out of your car and show it to them."

I went into Brookstone and a young man greeted me who obviously knew nothing about getting new products into the store, so he gave me the phone number for the corporate headquarters in New Hampshire. The next day, I called and found out the name of the purchasing guy, Steve Rich. He gave me the Sharper Image treatment and ghosted me for a few weeks but eventually called.

From out of nowhere, I was in my office one day when my secretary told me, "I've got a guy named Steve Rich on line two. He says he is from Brookstone. Do you want to take it?" Flabbergasted, I picked my jaw up off the floor and said, "Uh, yes, please!"

When I picked up, Steve told me, "Hey, every morning I get to my desk and I see a note that Bob Trussell from Tempur-Pedic pillows called. Would you please stop calling me?" That sure took the air out of my balloon. However, I stayed persistent. Sheepishly, I offered my last-ditch effort. "Yes, I apologize. I will stop calling you. But before I let you go, I want to make sure you've taken the pillow out of the box and squeezed it."

He replied, "Yes, it's a nice pillow, but I have no interest in putting it in our stores. I don't know what else to tell you. Do you want me to send it back?"

"No, just keep it." I hung up the phone and figured maybe

I should call Sharper Image for attempt number 10,001. Before getting too discouraged, I was reinvigorated, because about fifteen minutes later, the phone rang again. It was Steve Rich and he said, "You know, maybe I'll take this to research and see what we might be able to do with it."

My interpretation of what really happened is that he didn't take the pillow out of the box until after we got off the phone the first time. When he did and realized how superior the product was, he wanted to take it home, give it to his wife, get her opinion, sleep on it for a night or two, and let me know if it was something worth pursuing for his stores.

Two days later, he called me back and said, "You convinced me, but now I have to convince the purchasing board. If they come through, we'll talk about a deal."

A week later, he called and told me, "If you give us 100 floor models, we'll buy 400 pillows." That sounded like a good deal to me, so I signed off and we were in Brookstone shortly after.

The Tempur-Pedic pillow became the star of the show in Brookstone's stores. Once that happened, who do you think I heard from? That's right—the purchasing people from Sharper Image called because our pillows were flying off the shelves at their biggest competitor. They offered me a deal, saying they realized they won't get exclusive rights, but they didn't want to be undercut for price anywhere. I struck a deal with them that put Tempur-Pedic neck pillows in Brookstone and Sharper Image retailing for $90 in both stores.

A short period of time went by and Brookstone expressed how they weren't happy that we were selling the same pillows to their archrivals. I told the CEO of Brookstone, Mike Anthony, that we would take the pillows out of Sharper Image if they would sell our mattresses as well. Most Brookstone stores did not have a big floor space, so they didn't want a mattress taking up most of it. Nonetheless, the exclusivity for them on such a popular product (the pillow) was worth losing the floor space to display the mattress.

The mattress was indeed a space hog, but it worked. People bought the mattress *and* the pillow. Soon enough, Brookstone sold one or two mattresses per week and it was the hottest product in the store. *We were a big part of their sales and they were a big part of ours.*

OUR "EUREKA!" MOMENT

Despite our success in the chiropractors' offices and in retail, we still didn't know how to advertise the product on a mass scale. We had the entire United States to sell to but didn't know the best way to get the message out.

The company was growing at about 40 percent every year

throughout the early to mid-1990s. In the late 1990s, we began placing ads in *The New Yorker* magazine. The advertisement asked people to place a phone call to receive a free video that would show them all the wonderful benefits of our products. That initially garnered us about 25,000 calls, but we weren't selling enough mattresses from it to break even with the cost of the ads.

Just as I was thinking of pulling the ads and going in a different direction, someone from *The New Yorker* called me and said, "Bob, you're using an 800 number as a call to action in your advertising. That means you're eligible for our direct response rates." I replied, "What does that mean?" He said, "It means you can pay $6,000 for a one-page add that now costs you $25,000."

How I didn't know about that is beyond belief, but it was news to me and the rest of the company. Nobody had heard of the direct response rate card at *The New Yorker* before. It was also news to my advertising agency in Lexington, Kentucky. This was truly a eureka moment. We doubled our money almost instantly and got heavily involved in national advertising. The company went to another level of growth when we took full advantage of our exclusivity deal. And the rest, as they say, is history.

In 2003, we took the company public, and in 2012, we acquired another major player in the mattress industry,

Sealy. Although the companies continue to operate separately, we purchased their business for around $228 million.

It's almost been like a dream to think of my entrepreneurial journey, starting with those connections in the horse industry. One of the things I'm most proud of is Tempur-Pedic International employing over 6,000 people. That's a lot of jobs for good hardworking people who can create a nice life for themselves.

A SPECIAL THANKS

My life went through a complete turnaround when the horse industry collapsed. I will forever be grateful to John Gaines from Gainesway Farm who got me out of the not-so lucrative side of that industry and into the upper end of it, where I could make decent money.

John enabled me to execute international horse deals. Without that, I never would have met Alain the French horse trainer, who introduced me to C. G., the Swedish chiropractor, who eventually brought me to Mikael Magnusson. All those people were crucial to my success, and I'll never forget them for that. In your darkest of hours, there could always be a silver lining; you just have to keep looking.

MY ADVICE

Entrepreneurialism isn't for everybody. I think my story is a good indicator of how persistence is a must-have tool for the trade. A lot of people might have given up after coming up with an idea as ridiculous as selling mattresses to drivers at truck stops and having it blow up in their faces. Not everybody is willing to call a purchasing contact from a retail store thousands of times before getting a response. Also, when a lot of people realize they left a check for $50,000 on the floor of a fast-food restaurant, they might think that they're not cut out for this sort of thing. The truth is, you can't let obstacles and challenges stop you from doing what you want to do. Be persistent, take risks, and believe in the product and yourself.

Believing in the product is big. You need to know why you're better than the other options. Wait for a deal where you think you have an advantage; there needs to be some sort of barrier to entry for competition. If everybody can do what you're doing, they will, and you'll become irrelevant fast. Being the first mover is a good edge, but having a clear point of difference in your product or service is even better. We had a better mattress and pillow. Nobody else had what we had, so we were set up to succeed. All I had to do was execute. A big part of the reason I was able to execute was that I had inherent persistence going for me. My entrepreneurial journey included plenty of mistakes, but I believed in myself and my product. That was my key to success.

One last piece of information I think most entrepreneurs get stuck on is that maintaining control of your company is overrated. In the end, I owned only 5 percent of my company, but that didn't matter much. I had to keep selling to keep growing the company at various points of its evolution. You can scale only so much on your own. Of course, selling meant I received stock options, which became quite valuable as well, but that's not a big deal. *What was pivotal to my success was that the company kept growing. Would you rather own 100 percent of a bite-size pie or 5 percent of a football-stadium-size pie?* Think about that if you ever find yourself in a position when you're unwilling to give up a portion of control over your company. Don't be stubborn; do what's right for everybody.

"Would you rather own 100 percent of a bite-size pie or 5 percent of a football-stadium-size pie?"

PART 3

2017 INDUCTEES: DOUG COBB, KIMBERLY KNOPF, AND JOE STEIER

DOUG COBB

"Doug," my father said, "there are more than a million things you'll be able to do with your life. The only one you can't do is work for me." My father spoke those words of wisdom to me many years ago. To be fair, he also said them to my brother. I'm not sure I realized it at the time, but that sentiment set clear expectations for both of us. If we were going to make it in the world, we would need to do it on our own; we were told to figure things out for ourselves. Looking back, my entrepreneurial journey started right there.

I was born in California while my dad was a member of the Marine Corps. Louisville, however, was my mom's hometown, so when I was about three years old, my mom and dad decided to go back to her roots and we lived in Kentucky for my childhood and adolescence.

When I was around middle school age, my dad quit his full-time job and started his own business. A risky move? Some might see it that way, but he never did. Most importantly, he never showed it. His transition from full-time employee to American entrepreneur was so seamless that it seemed like he just stopped going to work one day and nothing else changed.

It was interesting for me to witness how matter-of-factly my father took responsibility for his own income. There was never any sense of panic, fear, or even a more-than-moderate level of concern about his choice to be his own boss. Watching the calmness and confidence he displayed in his everyday language and actions had a powerful impact on me. At a young age, I saw that working for yourself could be quite prosperous. I also saw that it didn't have to make you manic about where your next paycheck would come from or how you were going to pay the bills. What I learned was to believe in yourself, work hard, and make good decisions; the rest should take care of itself. The way my father conducted himself as an unruffled and self-assured businessperson became the catalyst for my entrepreneurial journey.

THE APPLE OF MY EYE

I continued to watch the way my father managed his business throughout my school years.

After graduating from high school, I went to Williams College in Massachusetts, where I received a bachelor's degree in political economy. Almost immediately after, I went to the New York University Stern School of Business to acquire my master's degree in accounting. Later on, I went to work for a company called Queue Corporation in Indianapolis, Indiana.

While working for Queue, my wife, Gena, and I bought an Apple II home computer with our tax refund in the springtime of 1980. In those days, it was considered state of the art. The now-iconic Apple II came in a variety of configurations. The one we had came with about a forty-character-wide monitor, a floppy disc drive, about 48k of memory, and 140k of storage. For an extra $350 later, we added 16k to produce a powerhouse 64k. Of course, those specs are laughable today. Adding 16k to any machine now would be virtually unnoticeable. Subsequently, just imagine how much memory $350 *would* buy in today's market.

At Queue Corporation, we met a gentleman by the name of Tom Cottingham. Tom was a great guy and became one of those people in my inner circle with a powerfully positive influence on my career trajectory. My wife, Tom, and

I began to publish material for the quickly emerging home computer market. Almost immediately, we saw profitable results from our "side hustle."

Once we saw money coming in and analyzed the long-term potential of the industry, we thought we may have been onto something, and we were right. We quit our day jobs at Queue and moved back to Louisville to start our own company. Thus, the Cobb Group was born.

THE COBB GROUP FLOURISHES WITH FOCUS

The original conception of the Cobb Company was to create multimedia for training and information related to desktop computing. At first, we thought we would publish books and newsletters, along with presenting live seminars at hotels and conference locations where we would teach people how to use various forms of software.

A few years after we started, we realized that there was only one solid business in that scope of services we were planning, which was the newsletters. So we sold off the book business, stopped doing the training seminars, and focused on the newsletters. With that renewed focus, the company flourished with tremendous growth.

Eventually, the Cobb Group became the world's leading publisher of newsletters for personal computer users. At its peak, we exceeded $20 million in annual revenues and employed over 150 people. Not bad for the initial investment of our 1980 tax refund.

After operating that business for about a decade, I thought, "Starting one innovative company and watching it grow was a lot of fun. Starting five of them, or maybe more, would be even more fun." With that in mind, we sold the business to Ziff Communications Company in 1991 for 200 times the return for its investors.

CHRYSALIS CRYSTALLIZES

When I decided to leave the Cobb Group, a good friend of mine, David Jones Jr., had just moved back to Louisville from Washington, DC. I was able to persuade him to join me in forming a venture capital firm called Chrysalis Ventures. Once David bought in, we invested our money into some of the most interesting and promising startups we could find. I did that for about three years before I was inspired and motivated to help one of our investments to achieve its enormous potential.

I couldn't help but be beyond impressed with two young founders—Mike Davis (who is also a Kentucky Entrepreneur Hall of Fame inductee and has his own chapter in this book) and Yung Nguyen. They had created a company with the idea to create a notification system that would alert victims of violent crimes anytime a dangerous individual, who posed a threat to their safety, had been released from custody.

Mike and Yung were obviously special people. Their problem wasn't to gather business; it was the opposite. Their company, called Appriss, Inc., was growing so fast that it reached a point where it needed a CEO with more marketing experience. This is not an uncommon occurrence for businesses with a rapid rise in growth.

With the company getting phone calls from all over the country to service various areas of law enforcement, Mike asked me to step in as CEO to guide the company through its growing pains. I believed so strongly in what they were doing and who they were as people that I didn't think twice about it. So I stepped in and served as the CEO of Appriss for about ten years. During that decade, Mike stayed with the company, served in various roles, and was my right-hand man. After all, it was his and his partner's innovation. Nobody knew the company like they did.

CHOOSE THE RIGHT RISK

An interesting dichotomy existed in the early days of Appriss. If one critical decision we made didn't turn out right, the company probably never would have made it. That's not unusual. In business, you have to take risks.

Studying the market carefully, trusting your instincts, and choosing the right risk is often the make-or-break moment for even the world's most game-changing ideas.

While Appriss was still in its infancy, long-distance telephone charges were down to around $0.19 per minute. (For all the millennials and Gen Zers out there, this information is correct. Cell phones didn't always exist and people would pay a rate to call beyond their local area from a landline telephone.) However, the industry was changing. Technology was breaking through that was steadily reducing the rate of long-distance charges. A few years prior, the cost was around $0.30 per minute.

A big part of Appriss's business model relied on using basic telephone lines to transmit data. This was the early days of the internet, which did not include high-speed fiber networks or broadband connections; data ran on POTS (plain old telephone service) lines.

Mike and I, along with other decision makers at Appriss saw the trend of long-distance rates decreasing. We also kept up with what was happening in the data world, so we knew that big companies were investing in ways to transmit data faster and cheaper all the time. Therefore, we made a big bet and assumed that long-distance rates would continue to fall.

If long-distance rates stayed at $0.19 per minute or fell

by only a marginal percentage, Appriss would have never made it. Lucky for us, our wager paid off. Ultimately, long-distance rates became nonexistent as the internet evolved to what it is today.

There were no guarantees that we were going to catch that break. If you're a business owner, there are no guarantees that you will catch the break you need for your company to take off either. But you have to assess the market, make an educated judgment call, and choose the right risk. It's not enough to just recognize variables in play; you must take action on what you think is right. What happens after that is out of your control, so don't look back. Something is going to have to break your way at some point. If it doesn't, there's always your next idea to get started.

GIVING BACK

When I look back at my entrepreneurial journey, it was a lot of fun. I enjoyed being a part of Chrysalis, Appriss, and many other startups. As much fun as it was to generate profits with those companies, I can honestly say that I've enjoyed what it's enabled me to do later in life even more; a big part of that is spending money on causes I care about.

For the last fifteen years, I've been on the board of South-east Christian Church, which has been an interesting and satisfying venture. Big churches can have a big impact in many different ways, so having a voice in deciding where Southeast Christian can help the community is an amazingly enjoyable experience for me.

Over the last few years, I've dedicated the majority of my time to The Finishing Fund, which is a venture capital fund whose mission is to get the gospel out to the farthest corners of the world. The Finishing Fund is actually a traditional venture capital model applied to a philanthropic endeavor. In the efforts to get the Word of God out to the world, there are two entities that need to connect. One is donors who desperately want to contribute to the cause but don't know how. The other are ministries that can spread the word but don't have access to the capital they need. Our role at The Finishing Fund is to connect those parties and form a pathway that increases humanity's relationship with their savior.

I'm fortunate to be able to apply the lessons I learned through my entrepreneurial journey to these causes I feel so closely connected to.

A SPECIAL THANKS

There have been many individuals who have intersected with my entrepreneurial path. I'd like to mention a few of them here, because I feel fortunate to have known them and consider many of them to be good friends.

Mike Davis and I became acquainted through our mutual business interests. As of the writing of this book, he and I still get together about once a month for breakfast and have great conversations. I am grateful for having known him for many years now. He is an amazing person and entrepreneur for several reasons. One of them is his eternal optimism. All Mike needs to know is that there's a chance something *can* work and he goes for it. Consequently, the idea usually ends up being a tremendous success.

Rarely in the business world does a founder step down from their leadership role and eventually step back in. But that's exactly what Mike did. In 2010, Mike took the CEO reins back from me, as I returned to Chrysalis as an Entrepreneur in Residence, and guided it to even more success over the next ten years before handing it off again to infinitely more capable hands. Today, Appriss remains one of the most exciting companies in all of Kentucky.

Another individual I want to extend a special thanks to is my colleague David Jones, Jr. David and I have been friends since childhood. I attribute a great deal of my success to my partnership with him at Chrysalis Ventures.

The thing I love and respect most about David is how differently he thinks from everybody else. Every time an issue came up in a business with which I was working, I would look at it from what I thought was every conceivable angle. I usually saw three or four different possibilities and figured I had to make a decision from those choices. If I then presented the issue to David, he would come up with a totally different perspective just about every time, one that I never would have thought of. Having that kind of unique insight on your team is invaluable; it allows you to innovate where others get stuck. David and I also remain good friends today.

Finally, I want to recognize Tom Cottingham who was indispensable in the success of the Cobb Group. Actually, I consider him to be a founder of that business, along with my wife and me. Tom was a marketing genius who helped us to figure out a lot of growing pains in the early days of the company.

Tom was a great joy to work with, and I cannot speak highly enough about his influence and the example he set. There is no doubt in my mind that he will be in the Kentucky Entrepreneur Hall of Fame one day as well, and (I hope) we'll be reading about him in a future volume of *Unbridled Spirit*.

MY ADVICE

Surrounding yourself with great people is something you'll see in every successful entrepreneur. If you're looking for a common bond with all the inductees to the Kentucky Entrepreneur Hall of Fame, I bet all of us would say that we had great people with whom to work. Find partners, supporters, and others who are equally committed to working hard and will support you. In the end, those people will prove to be your most valuable assets.

I would also say that focus is underrated. When we narrowed the Cobb Group from books and training courses to just newsletters, the business tripled. That was no coincidence. Call it addition through subtraction if you want, but the decision allowed us to put all of our energy behind one thing, which created maximum output. A lot of entrepreneurs try to hedge their bets by being everything to everybody, but my experience is that you'll end up being mediocre in all your efforts that way. If you narrow your focus, you can excel. Just keep telling yourself, "You got this."

Another valuable business lesson I've learned comes from my old days of flying airplanes. I don't do that anymore, but I always applied an old expression from that time, which was, "There are three things you can't use when flying a plane: the runway behind you, the altitude above you, and the fuel you left on the ground." It's another way of saying, "Take full advantage of the resources at your disposal. Don't waste time thinking about what you can't use." Raise capital and be careful about how you spend your resources.

Surround yourself with great people, narrow your focus, and spend wisely. From there, I'll draw inspiration from another expression that originates in the world of airplanes: the sky's the limit!

> "Surround yourself with great people, narrow your focus, and spend wisely. From there, I'll draw inspiration from another expression that originates in the world of airplanes: the sky's the limit!"

KIMBERLY KNOPF

My entrepreneurial journey began in Louisville, Kentucky when I was given an assignment in sixth grade to research "The American Dream."

Today's sixth-graders would do a quick Google search and come up with about 150,000 results from which they could pick and choose information. I had to do old-school research (just like every other twelve-year-old of that time). I perused a set of old hardcover encyclopedias to gather the necessary information. I think it might have been the *Encyclopedia Britannica*, but I'm not sure. The assignment turned out to be quite the eye-opener for a young mind in progress. Without knowing it, I was researching something that I would experience firsthand as an adult.

I wish I held on to that assignment, as I think it would not only be somewhat humorous for my friends and family to see today, but it would be interesting to see how I interpreted the subject at such a young age.

Later on, I went to Sacred Heart Academy in Louisville for high school. That turned out to be one of the best decisions my parents made for me. My four years there shaped and defined a lot of who I am today. Many of the relationships I made there are my lifelong friends whom I still talk with today.

My experiences at Sacred Heart proved critical to my development as a leader. I was committed to our student council and heavily involved with sports, which is a great learning opportunity for teamwork. Although I enjoyed a lot of sports, basketball was my game. It's no secret that I'm proud to have been a member of the 1976 Sacred Heart championship team. We played hard, worked together, and achieved our goal of being the best. Those are all lessons that can be applied to business as well.

I earned good grades throughout my early education and got accepted into the University of Kentucky (UK) for college. Ever since, I've been a big fan of the Wildcats, following Coach Cal (and hoping for another national championship soon). I sat out the first semester and worked two jobs to earn enough money for tuition. During the day, I worked at a bed and bath retail boutique, and at night I worked as a cashier at a grocery store.

An exceptional work ethic has always been a big part of who I am, and I attribute that to my parents and my upbringing. All five children attended Catholic schools and each of us worked to offset tuition. Once I started at UK, I participated on the student center board, held leadership roles in Alpha Gamma Delta sorority, and worked to pay for my tuition.

In the beginning of my time at UK, I didn't know exactly what I wanted to do, so I created my own major, which was a combination of courses that culminated in 1982 with a degree in international studies. From there, I proceeded to live my version of The American Dream for the next forty-plus years.

AN EARLY START

The American Dream didn't start immediately after college for me. My first postgraduate job was at a life insurance company called Northwestern Mutual. That experience was beneficial in a couple of ways. The first benefit was that I gained a deep understanding of sales. Perhaps the most profound benefit from that job was that I knew it was something I *didn't* want to do with the rest of my life.

Working in a cubicle or an office with a templated approach

to business was not my ideal situation. The environment wasn't as much of a problem as were the restrictions to my inherent spark for innovation. I wanted to be in a place where I could use my natural inclination toward creativity combined with my passion for customer service.

Soon enough, it dawned on me that I couldn't work for another company, not just yet. I had to at least try to do something that suited my passion and purpose, and the best way for me to do that would be to start my own business. No insurance company or large-scale enterprise was going to provide me with what I needed out of my career. In fact, nothing but being a decision maker in the systems and processes of my own entity would do.

With my entrepreneurial spirit beginning to take full flight at twenty-three years old, I set out to start a business where I could do all the things I wanted to do. I didn't have any capital of my own to make this happen, but I was fortunate that my soon-to-be husband, Ken, had a father and stepmother who cosigned a banknote for me to purchase the business that would become my milestone achievement as an entrepreneur. With their support and involvement, I opened my first Mattress Warehouse store in South Charleston, West Virginia in 1983.

Creativity was at the heart of my vision. I wanted to push that aspect of my mindset through marketing and displays of the products. I was young and driven, so those goals were just scratching the surface of the multitude of things I wanted to do. I really wanted to be involved in all the aspects of the company—marketing, customer service, accounting, deliveries, and even the loading and unloading of trucks. At one point, I strapped mattresses to the roof of my car to get them to where they needed to be.

No amount of work was off-limits for me in those days, as I worked seven days a week for a long time. If a customer had an issue with one of my products, I would get in the car and visit them in their homes to rectify the situation. To some, that might sound like an obsession, but to an entrepreneur, it's what drives us.

A FAMILY BUSINESS

In the beginning, the four of us—Ken, his father, step-mother, and myself—formed the business that would later become known as Innovative Mattress Solutions. Ken and I were married two years later, had our first daughter, Karrie, in 1986 and our second, Kristin, in 1990.

I soon realized that raising children as a female entrepreneur created unique challenges. There was no way that I could afford to take twelve weeks off for maternity leave while my business was still in the early stages of growth. When I had my first child, I did the company payroll from the hospital bed the next day. This isn't uncommon for women who are business leaders; we do what we have to do. Many of my employees had the same situation. It was a balancing act. To grow a business, there is no way to avoid a lot of travel to factories, conferences, stores, and other locations.

When my kids were young, I had a nursery set up in the store or the office sometimes. Ken and I combined daycare with babysitters for the occasional days when I had to take them to work with me. My kids grew up in the business. It was somewhat comforting and helpful that my VP of Finance had four children and shared those same challenges. In 1993, with nine stores, we implemented our point-of-sale computer system. We frequently brought our kids to the corporate office on nights and weekends. In the adjoining showroom, the kids sat on the beds and watched television while we worked. Of course, if you put any kid in a store full of mattresses, they are inevitably going to jump on them. On one occasion when I was working with a customer during a store visit, Karrie was jumping on a mattress, fell off, and broke her collarbone. Fortunately, Karrie recovered well from that incident and went on to become a highly successful woman. She worked in the family business for about ten years and most recently moved to Switzerland with her family. I'm extremely proud of both my girls, as Kristin has gone on to achieve her own success as well. Presently, she works in the Washington, DC area as a management and IT consultant.

GROWTH THROUGH ACQUISITIONS

During our first twenty years of business, we achieved a lot of success and I wanted to show appreciation to my team and vendors. The Knopf family decided to close the stores, warehouses, and corporate office so that everyone could celebrate our twenty-year milestone. Employees invited their spouses or companions. For a few days in November of 2003, our team enjoyed the lovely amenities provided by the Greenbrier Resort in West Virginia. We had a formal dinner with well over 150 attendees that was followed the next day by facilitated meetings. The purpose was for our team to pause and be grateful for our blessings during the Thanksgiving season. The gathering also served to get a consensus opinion regarding growth, which is always risky and requires capital and intense efforts from everyone.

I vividly remember those sessions and discussing the pros and cons of various scenarios of expansion. Several days later, at the age of forty-three, I drove away from the Greenbrier feeling refreshed and excited about the next phase of our journey.

From 2003 to 2012, the company completed five acquisitions, which increased the company's footprint from West Virginia to Kentucky, Ohio, Tennessee, Indiana, and Alabama. During those nine years, the company grew from 20 to more than 150 stores and added multiple warehouses to support distribution. The corporate office also moved from

West Virginia to Kentucky around this time. Sales, operations, and management staff grew exponentially as did marketing, inventory, and distribution budgets.

As I look back on those years, I always enjoyed onboarding and integrating the teams into our strong, family-oriented culture. It was hard work but something that was rewarding.

WHAT'S IN A NAME?

One of the early obstacles to the company's growth was the name. Unfortunately, the problem with the name was not some Shakespearian philosophical ponderance related to finding beauty. Just the opposite. Our name, Mattress Warehouse, was the subject of an ugly litigation case.

The result of the lawsuit was that the name Mattress Warehouse was intellectual property that we would not be allowed to use outside of West Virginia. To expand beyond that area, we had to change the name. So our team dreamed up the Sleep Outfitters brand.

Sometimes you lose the battle but win the war. Although we lost a rather lengthy court battle, a bizarre turn of events happened soon after, as a series of complexities hovered over the entire situation, the depth of which is too involved to accurately depict in this short synopsis. What I can provide is a summary of the results.

The person who sued us over the company name passed away. His brother took over the business and evidently wasn't terribly interested in holding on to it, so he approached us with an offer for us to buy him out. That's right. The same company that just defeated us in a court battle was now seeking us to acquire it. Only in America!

At first, I denied the request, as it seemed as absurd as it was confounding when thinking about the chaos we endured from the lawsuit. When I had time to really think about it, though, logic won me over. By acquiring that company, we would have an immediate point of entry to the Ohio market. We eventually agreed to the deal, which led to further acquisitions and our unprecedented growth.

NEW HORIZONS

My entrepreneurial journey came a long way from that first store, where I did almost everything including turning the lights on and off every morning and evening. Throughout the company's growth, we continued our mission to make the world better by helping people get a better night's sleep. My vision was always to align our people, products, and partners to put forth an exceptional customer experience. I believe we made good on that promise to our customers, and I'm proud of how we accomplished so much over my three-plus decades at the helm.

Around 2017, I started to think of what I wanted to do in the next chapter of my life. Over the next two years, I began recruiting people who could take over my role in the business. Finally, I stepped away in 2019 to work on my new company, New Horizons Franchise Group.

Entrepreneurs helping other entrepreneurs has always been something in which I've believed. It's one way I can marry my passion with purpose. At New Horizons Franchise Group, we help people to select a franchise, secure the funding they need, and get it launched.

I will always remember what it was like to be twenty-three years old with a dream but have no idea how to get it started. That confusion, especially for newer entrepreneurs, hasn't changed. So many people have the drive, passion, and innovation to be successful and impact the world, but they need a place where they can work with someone who knows what it takes to implement their vision. That's what we do at New Horizons, and I'm excited to see where this next phase of my entrepreneurial journey will go.

A SPECIAL THANKS

My business has always been centered on the relationships of those closest to me. Innovative Mattress Solutions, Sleep Outfitters, Mattress Warehouse, and all of the companies we acquired were family businesses, where my husband

and oldest daughter worked for many years. I also had two brothers who significantly contributed to the business with their hard work. Of course, without Ken's father and stepmother, we probably never would have had the funding we needed even to get started in the mattress business. The entire family has always been extremely supportive of the company. With the right people around you, as an entrepreneur, you never have to go it alone. My family has been amazing throughout the entire journey.

Some outstanding people have worked with me, and I still consider them to be extended family. Without their dedication and hard work, none of what I achieved would be possible. Until now, my only way to say thank you was by trying to provide enjoyable workspaces, where a work-family balance was always encouraged and good benefits could enable people to live well. Now I would like to seize this opportunity to extend my gratitude—in print form—to all of the wonderful people who were there for the ride.

The mattress industry was always highly competitive. If I didn't have the best talent in the world all around me, aligned with the idea of serving the customer in the best way possible, we never could have enjoyed the success we achieved. Thank you to anyone who was a part of that amazing history!

MY ADVICE

The entrepreneurial journey is never traveled on a smooth path. You need to endure the bumps in the road. Do your homework and abandon your fears of failure that will creep in from time to time. The best way to stare down all those challenges is to find a good support system (could be family, friends, colleagues, anybody) and find experienced, successful mentors. Learn from whoever you can to push forward on your path to success.

And so, I was a member of the West Virginia chapter of the Young Presidents' Organization (YPO) for fifteen years. The WVYPO is an international organization that supports the development of company presidents. I also joined the Lexington Vistage Chapter, which like YPO, provided education and support to business leaders and owners.

Getting started is likely the hardest thing for most entrepreneurs. That's a big reason why I love my work with New Horizons Franchise Group so much. I get to show people how to get started. While doing so, I mentor people of all ages.

One aspiring businessperson is just nineteen years old and fresh out of high school. He certainly has the drive and ambition, as well as the creative mindset to make his dreams happen. If I can help him to get started, I know he'll do great things. I'm also currently working with a woman who used to work for me with Innovative Mattress Solutions. She has been saving for eight years to start her own company, and there is no doubt in my mind that she will achieve that dream.

These people I'm currently working with, and others, have made me realize that entrepreneurship has no age limits. You're never too young or too old to get started. I was quite young when I began my career and faced many obstacles, but those will be present for an entrepreneur at any age.

No matter what stage your business life is at, enjoy the journey. There will be long hours, difficult relationships, failed endeavors, and various levels of disappointment. But if you can ride it out, the rewards are satisfying and fulfilling like nothing else. You'll work with amazing people, have opportunities to give back to the community, and feel a tremendous sense of empowerment and accomplishment. *Entrepreneurship is a rewarding, fulfilling, and satisfying journey. Get started, pivot when you need to, and enjoy all the possibilities that come from living The American Dream!*

> "Entrepreneurship is a rewarding, fulfilling, and satisfying journey. Get started, pivot when you need to, and enjoy all the possibilities that come from living The American Dream!"

JOE STEIER

I think I was given an unfair advantage (or two) in life as a young child. Not only was I born in the great city of Louisville, Kentucky, but I was also adopted by two amazing parents. That's right. I think adoption gave me an edge in becoming who I am today.

It seems like there is a higher ratio of adopted business leaders and founders compared to the general population. Keep in mind that I have zero scientific proof of that, but I know what I see and feel, and I have some personal experience to back that opinion.

Many of my mother's sisters had adopted children as well, so I'm *not* the only adopted person in my family. The interesting thing is that many of us share this unusually strong attachment to things like mission and vision, both strong traits of entrepreneurialism.

Grit in adopted children seems to be an undeniable trait. The reason could be that perhaps some level of psychological rejection exists in us on a subconscious level. My parents always loved and supported me, so my environment provided me with everything I needed to be successful. However, I feel like an element of rejection might be ingrained into a lot of adopted kids that turns us into overachievers. Many of us can't help but feel like we need to prove our abilities, strength, and determination to an even greater level than kids from more traditional family dynamics. What does this mean to me? If you're an entrepreneur and you're adopted, I'll bet on you any day!

THE ENTREPRENEURIAL JOURNEY IS NEVER A LINEAR PATH

I was intrigued by entrepreneurs at a young age. When I was growing up, a lot of kids had a newspaper delivery route, but I had multiple routes. I figured, "Use the multiplier effect. If a kid can make so much money on one route, I'll make double that if I can do two routes. What if I did more?" The possibilities for more were always churning in my brain.

As I got older, I was always the guy that would go to the nearby gas station and talk to the owner about how they bought their business. The idea of controlling my destiny always appealed to me. If I wanted to keep learning, do more, and have impact, I knew I needed the sage advice of others who had already been there and done that.

I made money by whatever means I could as a kid, an adolescent, and a young adult. My first real experience as a business owner started in my early twenties when I owned a bar that was founded by my grandfather, started a comedy wake-up service, purchased flower shops, and always bought real estate every chance I could get. Although neither of those early businesses would be where I would find my destiny, they were still the beginning of an amazing journey of learning. The comedy wake-up service actually had great media exposure hitting several business covers quickly and the bar won several national awards, so I enjoyed some success early in my career and still own that neighborhood bar today as well as much of the original real estate acquisitions. Right when you think you figure it out, adversity always crosses our path, as it inevitably will for all of us and that is when the fire burns hotter or burns out.

Nobody's entrepreneurial journey is a linear approach. You must have grit; further, you must be willing to take the occasional detour when you're knocked off your initial chosen path. Be adaptable and willing to discover new territory. Greater lessons are always learned through resiliency and tenacity than with unchallenged complacency.

Still in my mid-twenties, I attempted to build off my initial success by embarking on a joint retail shopping development with a partner. Unfortunately, I didn't do enough homework in that situation. If I would have read the city documents about the site, I would have understood the road repairs that were coming.

After we built the site and our retailers moved in, the city tore up the roads surrounding the development. It made access highly undesirable for any consumer to want to do shopping in our shiny, new, expensively built shopping center. Consequently, the retailers made no money, which led to them not making their lease payments or closing up, which led to me and my partner losing a ton of money. That sent me back to my parents' basement to live.

That was a big hit for me. It made me see who my real friends were for sure and how faith and family must be your foundation. I went back to my faith looking for answers, one of which was abundantly clear: *work harder.* I already had a good job as a CPA and added two side hustles along the way because I refused to give up or ever quit my dreams. I feel like too many people expect entrepreneurialism to be a linear path. They quit when they hit an especially big bump in the road that gives them a flat tire. Fix the flat, get back in the car, and keep going.

LEARNING FROM FAILURE

Society often misinterprets failure as purely negative. Whereas none of us start out wanting to fail, it should be seen as a prerequisite to sustainable success. Failure is an opportunity to learn. I reflected on my failures, made note of where things went wrong, and rejuvenated my entrepreneurial journey almost right away.

My previous experience was not a destination; it was part of a much larger journey. I needed to keep learning, keep building on my track record, and keep getting better. Around the mid-1990s, I bought into a Louisville-based pizza restaurant chain called Bearno's with close friends. We still all own that as a group and it's still a great company with a forty-five-year history of accolades. Heck, we were in China before Papa John's was! Those steady, entrepreneurial team-based experiences keep me prepared for bigger things.

In 1997, I co-founded a successful healthcare consulting firm called Professional Healthcare Services (PHS) that did some breakthrough work, reaching twenty-three states. With the feeling fresh in my mind that I needed to keep learning, keep moving, and keep building, I started to get into more real estate ventures and discovered my passion for healthcare transformations. Then I became a third partner, President, and Chief Operating Officer (COO) of Home Quality Management, Inc, which was a national turnaround success. That role lasted for about eight years, until it was sold and it was my time for my signature (pardon the pun) contribution to the entrepreneurial world, where I could try to put it all together in an impactful way.

BUILDING MISSION INTO LONG-TERM CARE

Signature HealthCARE was born from an innate feeling I've had for as long as I can remember. As an adopted child, I always felt an undeniable connection to nonfamily as well as those closest to me. This compassion was unexplainable for a long time, but as an adult with the hindsight of many years and lessons learned behind me, I became better equipped to make more sense of it.

Back in high school, I began volunteering at nursing homes. I saw other kids my age come and go, residents who decided they didn't want help anymore, and of course, plenty of residents who passed away. In other words, I got used to losing people. I don't mean that to sound trite in any way, but it had a significant impact on my desire to change things that I didn't think were working well in the long-term care space.

It's strange how negative outcomes like failure, loss, and others can lead to motivation. I never forgot that feeling of loss. It stayed with me past high school and into my adult years. As an entrepreneur, I held on to it as a motivation for change.

I set out to build a national nursing home company with a focus on transformation. Nursing homes always had a tired stigma associated with them. They were places that provided no real benefit to enhancing the lives of their residents. Sure, their time on this earth was limited, but that didn't mean their final years needed to be spent wasting away in a bed with little to no quality of life.

"What if I could use my vision to create a franchise with a mission that creates more than the traditional model of long-term care facilities?" The idea was such an exciting endeavor for me to begin. I couldn't wait to get started, so I didn't wait. That's sort of a thing with me.

My belief is that we all have a special calling when we're younger about purpose; it could happen when we get older too, but I feel like most of us get it when we're in our formative years; we just need to recognize it. For me, adding to the quality of life and diminishing the negative impact of loss was an extremely rewarding and fulfilling mission to pursue as an entrepreneur. Thus, in 2007, I helped co-found Signature HealthCARE while leading them as President and Chief Executive Officer (CEO) for the past fifteen years.

THREE PILLARS

Signature HealthCARE was built with three pillars in mind: innovation, spirituality, and learning. The three pillars

aren't in any specific order, as each one is just as important as the other.

Our first pillar was to build an intrapreneurship pillar, where
our leaders could start companies within our company to
expand entrepreneurial access to other Signature leaders.
This was a somewhat revolutionary concept. This pillar has
built many successful spin-off companies that were either
sold or still thrive today, which shows how much entrepreneurship can be a competency taught and fostered for the
benefit of all.

Spirituality is another pillar at Signature HealthCARE. I've
always felt compelled to bring God into the workplace in a
big way. When I almost lost my own son, it was the peers
around me who helped me survive and create a miracle
healing that I continue to cherish every day. It's not necessary to be preachy, but I think it's important for people
to have spiritual resources where they can explore their
relationship with God. This is important at home and in
our careers. We believe you should be able to nurture your
faith wherever you are. I even went on my own spiritual
pilgrimage to the Holy Land, where I co-published a local
bestselling book, *My GOD! Our God?* The book embodies
the sacred journeys that we all walk.

The third pillar that rounds out our mission is learning. This
one is special to me because I know what it's like to face

challenges. I had severe dyslexia and struggled mightily throughout high school. As a kid, it was tough to face these challenges, but because of my inherent drive to improve myself, I eventually got a CPA, CNA, and MBA from Miami, as well as a master's and a doctorate in organizational learning from the University of Pennsylvania.

In our learning programs at Signature HealthCARE, we've helped people go from having a high school General Equivalency Degree (GED) to getting master's degrees in nursing and other healthcare-related fields. We've also won many national awards in learning under the "Leaders as Teachers" framework.

Our legacy from these three pillars remains a fundamental part of our mission at Signature HealthCARE—one that I'm extremely proud of and intend to promote for as long as possible.

A SPECIAL THANKS

There is no question that the biggest role model in my life has been my father. Early in his life, he was a bricklayer by trade. At some point, he wanted to have a real impact in the world, so he became a director of an apprenticeship program that went into the inner cities of Kentucky and the poverty-stricken rural areas of Appalachia to teach people skills that could help them to earn a good living.

My father always encouraged me to think bigger, not in terms of making money but in life. He also constantly preached the difference between a person of wealth and a person of independence. It was his own version of the "teach a man to fish" lesson from the Bible. He had a highly anti-corporate mindset and taught me to measure success not by the income I could generate but by the number of lives I could impact in a positive manner. Watching the way he conducted himself made me want to be both an entrepreneur and a teacher like he was.

There were three others who were instrumental in shaping my entrepreneurial journey after my father built the foundation.

Bruce Lunsford—with two other partners—founded a company called Vencor (originally called Vencare, now called Kindred Healthcare), which operated long-term, acute-care hospitals across the country. When I was a young person, Bruce took me under his wing and allowed me to pick his brain about entrepreneurship. Bruce was a great mentor to many. He allowed me to learn so much just by observing the way he built companies, and we are still close today.

Another pivotal piece to my entrepreneurial journey was George Friebert. George was a successful entrepreneur in Louisville who backed my initial venture into the healthcare industry at PHS. He showed me how to build a professional organization, not just a small business. Sadly, George passed away at a young age, but he was a phenomenal leader and extremely generous with his time, wisdom, and capital.

One of the founders of Humana, David Jones, Sr., was another incredible resource for young entrepreneurs in the Louisville area. Once a month, he gave me the chance to go deep on learning from him about what it takes to build an exceptional organization. David would teach me from the words of the legendary management consultant Peter Drucker. He would show me how various business models worked. David did this with me for about two and a half years, but I wasn't the sole beneficiary of his wisdom, as he was famous for helping local entrepreneurs and others in the Louisville community to consistently strive for better. He did it in a humble way, but he gave back a lot and strongly demonstrated what it means to be a true entrepreneur.

MY ADVICE

One thing I've learned from my mentors and my own experience is that there's no time like the present to get started. Sure, I began my journey at a young age, but why not get as much knowledge early on as you possibly can. Don't wait! I started quickly, failed fast, and leveraged my missteps into what would become great successes.

If you have ideas and a strong will to keep getting better, don't wait for an opportunity to come to you; make it happen! The sooner you can immerse yourself into the world of making decisions, the quicker you can make a difference. If you want to be an entrepreneur, do it now!

A big key to being a successful entrepreneur is to get a good mentor. Look around and find people who are not just successful but also embody the type of person and leader you want to become. Observe those people carefully and emulate them to a point. Be your own person, but don't be afraid to learn from the positive traits of others.

One more thing: Occasionally, I get down about the state of the world, which inevitably happens to all of us. It's part of the human condition as leaders who walk out front! When I feel I'm in a negative space, I go to events held by Awesome Inc. When I do that, I realize I don't have to worry about the next generation because they are as fired up as we were. We're going to be just fine in the future. I love what Awesome Inc does because they inspire people to be better. At their board meetings, I get to hear the stories of amazing leaders whom I have admired for decades. Further, I watch them and how they bestow their wisdom on younger generations, and I know that their words will be carried forward into future amazing entrepreneurial journeys like mine and yours.

"If you have ideas and a strong will to keep getting better, don't wait for an opportunity to come to you; make it happen! The sooner you can immerse yourself into the world of making decisions, the quicker you can make a difference. If you want to be an entrepreneur, do it now!"

PART 4

2018 INDUCTEES: DON BALL, SR., JESS CORRELL, JOE CRAFT, AND JIM HEADLEE

DON BALL, SR.

Honorary recollection by wife, Mira Ball.

Born of humble beginnings on a farm in Henderson County, Kentucky, Don Ball, Sr. grew up with one brother and two sisters. The kids were raised to have strong values, tireless work ethics, and never-ending compassion. They were taught a selfless and honorable way of life by their father, James Chester Ball, because of their mother's unfortunate passing when Don was four years old.

Don attended the local public school system, which was supported solely by county taxes. Henderson County was not a wealthy area, so the schools did not have much of a budget with which to work. As a result, the schools were lacking in resources and didn't bring out the academic potential in Don and many of the other kids.

Fortunately for Don, he had two big things going for him: one was the fact that he never quit. As a student or a businessperson, the idea of giving up never crossed his mind. The second thing he had going for him was that his Aunt Dee, on his dad's side, was 100 percent determined to help Don get into whatever college he wanted.

Dee, who was a teacher in Louisville, had a husband and a child who both sadly passed away, which was a big part of why she became dedicated to ensuring Don's well-being. He never forgot that, as he took great care of her in her elderly years to show his undying gratitude.

Aunt Dee took exceptional measures to encourage Don to go to school. A local businessperson, James S. Priest, also took him under his wing and provided guidance. James brought Don to Lexington and introduced him to some people at the University of Kentucky (UK). Evidently, that was enough to convince a young Don Ball to attend school there in the fall.

DESTINY FOUND AT THE UNIVERSITY OF KENTUCKY

Tuition at UK was $65 per semester in 1954, which helped

kids with Don's ambition and intellect to get a good start in life. Sadly, much of that situation doesn't exist anymore, as today's youth are expected to pay more than $50,000 per year to get a good education, often planting their feet firmly in debt's doorway before they even get started. The American dollar also went a lot further in those days, but Aunt Dee continued to help Don stay in school by sending him $20 a week to support himself.

As a high school student, Don got involved with the Future Farmers of America (FFA) and won many awards for his participation in the organization. At the time, UK had an excellent teacher in the agriculture department who made an impact on Don. So he decided to major in that field. He was also interested in political science but eventually switched over to the Commerce College for Business.

Don met his future wife, Mira, during the fall of his freshman year when they both attended the Baptist Student Union. They married just a couple of years later in 1955.

Don fell fifteen hours short of finishing school, while Mira held on and graduated with a degree in business education in 1956. Later on, many people questioned why Don didn't finish his degree. He usually answered by saying that the piece of paper meant nothing to him. He was happily married, had a beautiful family, and a wildly successful business. With those thoughts in mind, it's hard to argue anything else.

THE FAMILY BUSINESS BEGINS AND GROWS

With Mira by his side, the couple quickly formed a partnership in life and business, as they started a real estate venture while still attending UK. The couple bought, renovated, and sold houses. One distinction from today's "flippers" was that the family actually lived in the houses while renovating them. Don and Mira looked at real estate as providing a place to live while using sweat equity to leverage a profit. Business was good for the young couple, as they moved thirteen times in the first two and a half years of their marriage.

In 1959, Don and Mira formally named their business, Ball Homes. Shortly after, their business was given a chance for growth when a good friend of theirs was called into military service. Their friend was in the middle of building seven or eight houses at the time and asked Don to finish them. They were small homes for first-time buyers, which aligned perfectly with the original business model of Ball Homes. Making the most of the opportunity, Don finished the houses and made enough money to establish credit. That allowed the couple to buy more lots and start building more homes. The business had officially taken off.

When a section of Lexington called Cardinal Valley opened up, Don and Mira bought fifteen lots for about $2,700 each. At the same time, another builder had bought a group of more expensive sites. That builder had the recent Mrs.

America competition winner coming in to do a grand opening for his properties. Don capitalized on that marketing opportunity and made sure his houses were finished on the same day. By having the homes ready to show, Don and Mira would reap the benefits of traffic from the other builder's event. The strategy worked, as every lot was sold by the end of that weekend.

While their business was hitting its stride, the couple bought an office space and made a great team, where they focused on their individual strengths to optimize the business's efficiencies. Don was the deal man and the builder, while Mira took care of all the details. She handled the bookkeeping and paying the bills.

Ball Homes never sought the purchase of expensive lots to maximize profit. Maintaining lessons taught by his father about compassion for others, Don always wanted to build homes where the local police officers, firefighters, teachers, construction workers, and other middle-class citizens could afford to buy and sustain a good life for their families.

Under Don's leadership, the couple bought and sold numerous properties with this mission and vision for many years. They ran a highly profitable business while enabling a comfortable life for themselves and others. Growing the business from that stage required the combined efforts of the next generation of entrepreneurs in the family.

Don credited his children for taking the business from strictly a first-time home builder company to Central Kentucky's leading home builder and one that has ranked among the top 100 home builders in America every year since 1998. The company remains a family business today, as all three kids have played a pivotal role in growing the business to reach its lofty heights in the late 1990s and beyond. The one-time, two-person show now features a development branch, mortgage services, a property management team, and a real estate office.

When Don realized that his children were taking Ball Homes to new heights, he was granted the peace of mind to focus mostly on his nonprofit work. Thus, he moved his office to the family's 600-acre piece of land known as Donamire Farm, where he enjoyed the serenity and beauty of the natural surroundings to concentrate on giving back to the community.

BUILDING HOPE

Don always had a heart for helping people and believed strongly in giving people second chances. He was a big supporter of several worthy and meritorious charitable organizations, including the Alzheimer's Association, American Cancer Society, Big Brothers and Big Sisters of America, United Way, and The Salvation Army. He had a heart of gold and cared deeply for helping those organizations, but more than any other philanthropic endeavor, he wanted to build affordable housing for people who needed it most.

Interesting fact: If you look up Don Ball on Wikipedia, his page is titled Don Ball (Philanthropist). That says a lot about his generosity and spirit for helping others. He formed one of the biggest home-building companies in the nation, but philanthropy is listed as his most noteworthy title.

Because Don knew how to build affordable homes, he identified homelessness as a problem for which he could craft impactful solutions. When he dug a little deeper into the roots of homelessness, he saw that drug and alcohol addiction were the two biggest catalysts. As stated earlier, Don wanted to help people get a second chance after making a wrong turn or two in their lives. He soon got involved by finding lots and getting them cleared with Habitat for Humanity. This was right in his wheelhouse; he always had a knack for identifying areas in which to build. By doing it in a way that could help solve the homelessness problem, he combined his expertise in home building with his passion for helping people. It was a win-win for the community and him.

To get all those moving pieces together would be a herculean task for most people, but Don made it work. Ernie Fletcher was the governor of Kentucky at the time, and he appointed Don as the Head of Housing for the state. Don also served in the Kentucky House of Representatives from 1964 to1969. By leveraging his political presence, he was able to secure more money for addiction recovery and other nonprofits. From there, he established seventeen recovery centers across the state that help people to cleanse themselves from substance abuse and get their lives back in order.

Later in life, Don got the Justice and Health and Welfare cabinets together to do something similar to Habitat for Humanity. By getting those political allies to support his efforts, he was able to get homes built with tax credits and grants from the federal government. The homes were used as Section Eight housing, where people would agree to live in lieu of going to jail for drug possession. They never paid anything, but they had to agree to get sober; not a bad deal for those with the drive to make a better life for themselves and their families.

The Hope Center was built in 1993 as the first of its kind in addiction recovery services. Based in Lexington, the facility provided a comprehensive list of benefits for homeless and at-risk people to not only get food and shelter but also receive assistance with recovery, employment opportunities, and more.

A SPECIAL THANKS

The business and the charitable efforts would likely never have been possible if Don hadn't had an exemplary role model to follow as a youth. Don thought a lot of his father. He had good reason, as James Chester Ball raised four kids by himself at a time when most fathers would have run from such a challenge.

In his adult years, Don had other supporters who were influential in helping his career and life to prosper. Homer Hale, for example, was a mortgage banker who helped Don to continue building affordable housing during challenging economic times. During the Carter administration, interest rates hovered near 20 percent, which made it quite difficult for any middle-class citizen (Don's target demographic) to buy homes. Homer worked tirelessly to find creative ways to piece together mortgages that would enable people to buy houses without suffocating them financially.

There were others who had a significant influence on Don's career. Austin Sims was the Head of Housing while Don served in the state legislature. Together, they worked out a deal to secure a US Department of Housing and Urban Development (HUD) grant to knock down an impoverished neighborhood, where a lot of drugs were being sold, and rebuild it to provide affordable housing for honest, hard-working people. Governor of Kentucky at the time, Ernie Fletcher got Don appointed to local government, which enabled him to network with people who had influence and were able to push many philanthropic efforts through the red tape of government. That single act did a lot of good for Kentucky.

HIS ADVICE

Don Ball, Sr. passed away on March 23, 2018. His legacy lives on, however, in the causes he cared about most and in today's leadership at Ball Homes. Don and Mira's oldest son, Ray, is the President of the company; their second son, Mike, is in charge of construction; and their daughter, Lisa, is in charge of sales and rental management.

Entrepreneurs looking to draw inspiration from Don's journey need to look no further than the words given by then-Lexington Mayor Jim Gray: "Don Ball was a modern-day Horatio Alger. Truly the self-made man." There is no doubt that Don was a self-made man, but he never lost the common touch or his heart for those less fortunate. For those unfamiliar with the works of Horatio Alger, he wrote over 100 books, mostly about impoverished boys and their rise to prosperity. Don epitomized this story of success in many ways. He discovered his partner in life and business, Mira, raised a successful family, built a prolific career, and never forgot where he came from. He lived a life of generosity and success—not just from a financial perspective but through the betterment of humanity.

Don was never the type to lecture people with unwanted advice. He was a much better listener than someone who told people to do this or do that. Yet, *many lessons can be learned from Don's journey by the astute entrepreneur of today. He worked hard, never gave up, and always felt compelled to give back.*

"Many lessons can be learned from Don's journey by the astute entrepreneur of today. He worked hard, never gave up, and always felt compelled to give back."

JESS CORRELL

 I grew up in Somerset, Kentucky, about thirty minutes from where I now live in Stanford. My parents were strong Christians and amazing people. As the middle child of seven kids in a farming family, I like to joke that I turned out about as bad as I possibly could have, considering the parents I had and the brothers and sisters I grew up around. I was blessed with just about the best family anybody could ask for.

Mom and Dad took all of us to church regularly. They taught us early in life to read the Bible every day and to tithe everything we made. Giving was at the heart of their values and a core part of their joy. Their acts of generosity influenced me and became the start of my generosity journey.

Entrepreneurship was a big part of my dad's life. He told me, "When you start working for yourself, you make less than everybody around you. But later in life, you'll make much more."

Dad always encouraged us to work together on the farm. We helped with the cows and the garden. My first business venture was selling watermelons with my brothers when we were young. Dad was the epitome of an entrepreneur. He expanded into a bit of everything. He partnered with his brother on a used car lot, developed real estate, owned shopping centers, and later became a Shell jobber.

Perhaps the best piece of advice my dad gave me was about people. He said, "People are like elevators—they'll take you up and they'll take you down. You will become the composite of the five people with whom you spend the most time."

One day, my father drove this point home when we made a visit to his shopping center. While he took care of business, I stopped into a pool room he rented to a small business owner. I loved to play the pinball machines, but my dad didn't know that's where I was spending my time.

On this particular day, he found me inside the pool room and grabbed me by the ear. He turned me around to catch a good view of the cast of characters hanging out in there. "Look around, son," he said. "Is there anyone in this place you want to be like?" He dragged me out of that place by the ear and gave me a swift kick when we got outside. That incident made a big impression on me. I took his words to heart and became determined to spend my time a little more wisely going forward.

ENTREPRENEURIAL BEGINNINGS

Around the same time, I embarked on my first entrepreneurial venture with my older brother Kirk. We bought two Coca-Cola machines in Dad's shopping center. Once a week, we took the money out of the machines and put it in the bank. It wasn't much, but it was more than what most teenagers had in those days. When Kirk went to college, my brother Vince bought his interest and came into the picture as my partner. Although Vince and I also invested in some cattle earlier, the Coke machines were our first real business partnership.

Between my junior and senior years in high school, I decided to sell Bibles door to door in Waycross, Georgia. That was truly a transformative experience that taught me to deal with rejection and to not give up. It was in the middle of summer and hot as blazes. I got there as a 185-pound football player with hair down to my shoulders. I came home with a buzz haircut and about thirty pounds less weight.

While we were both in college, Vince and I met someone

who bought diamonds and sold them to his friends who were getting married. For college-aged kids, this sounded like a good business plan. Inspired by our friend's success, Vince and I found a wholesale jewelry magazine and looked for the biggest ad in the publication. We figured that would be a good place to buy diamonds and found an advertisement for Harry Winston, based in New York City. That was all we needed to convince ourselves to head to New York and begin our venture.

After going to gemology school, we started buying diamonds from Harry Winston and sold them to our friends who were getting engaged. Vince liked that business more than I did, so he decided to run its operations. Our partnership eventually included eleven jewelry stores throughout Kentucky, a wholesale company in Somerset, and a buying office in Bombay, India.

BUYING MY FIRST BANK

While Vince was running the jewelry business, I started running around with Lawrence Barnett, an experienced land trader down in Wayne County, Kentucky. We traded for all kinds of things including guns and antiques but primarily land. Over about four years, we accumulated around 8,000 acres of paid-for timberland. With those assets as collateral, I tried to buy my first bank with the help of Vince, Dad, and my uncle Blaine.

We missed our first two attempts. It did not help our cause that I didn't know much, if anything, about banking. My good friend Alton Blakely recommended that I hire a bank consultant and told me to go speak with a friend of his named Randy Attkisson. Randy was just the person I needed since he was a former State Banking Commissioner and had experience in owning and acquiring community banks.

In 1982, we bought Lincoln County National Bank in Stanford, Kentucky. I was twenty-six years old. Dad signed the note for us. I asked him who was going to run the banks. He said, "You are," to which I replied, "I don't know anything about running banks." He told me, "I know lots of bankers. You will do just fine."

I hired Randy as my consultant, which made sense. Later on, I hired him to become my Chief Executive Officer (CEO). He is still on our board today and remains a big shareholder. We bought a new bank about every two years. Vince was growing the jewelry business while I focused on banking.

In our youth, all Vince and I set out to do was become rich. We were not thinking about charitable giving or serving others as much as building our businesses. Despite our single- minded focus on business, we were still heavily influenced by our faith and the values our parents had instilled in us. As time went by, Vince became heavily involved with the ministry side of life.

AN EPIPHANY ABOUT MONEY

As Vince began to feel a calling to love and serve others, Dale Ditto introduced us to the Crown small group study, written by Howard Dayton, about biblical principles to finances. I told Dale that I needed help in every area of life except that one. Nonetheless, in the winter of 1992, six of our company executives decided to go through this study together. At that time of our lives, we owed around $21 million on our banks, real estate endeavors, and the jewelry company.

Before this study, Vince and I would borrow money wherever we could find it and buy just about anything we thought would make money. But we learned that there are over 2,300 verses in the Bible that mention money. The Bible encourages us to reduce debt, save more, give more, and place little value on material things. We realized we had been living our lives by nearly the opposite ideals. We decided to make some dramatic changes and got serious about getting out of debt as soon as possible. Five years later, we were debt-free and invested the extra income back into our business.

AN EPIPHANY ABOUT LIFE

As a businessperson in American society, we are taught to grow and expand—work harder and longer. I worked eighty hours a week, did not take vacations, and always strived for more of everything. As a result, my first wife left and took our three kids. It was a difficult time personally. This wake-up call forced me to make changes in my life.

The first weeks after my wife left, I had the kids for most of the summer. I instantly gained a deep appreciation for single mothers and a deeper appreciation for my own kids. I went from working eighty hours a week to forty. I used to read *The Wall Street Journal*, *Forbes*, *Fortune*, and a few of the local newspapers on a daily basis. All that became unimportant when I needed to spend time with the kids, cook, do laundry, and keep up the house. As hard as it was at the time, it was one of the best things that happened to me.

An unexpected part of that lifestyle changed: my business didn't suffer at all. In fact, losing my obsession allowed it to prosper. I had more time to think clearly, rather than getting distracted by all the outside influences in the news, financial markets, and everything flying around the business landscape. Becoming less obsessed with making money and more focused on life and family made me a better person *and* a better business owner.

A few years after my wife left, Vince was diagnosed with

an aggressive brain tumor and died within months at the age of thirty-eight. We were business partners until the end.

The next year, I met Angela. We both come from farming families and are seventh-generation Kentuckians. More importantly, we share our faith. She is my best friend and advisor. She went through the Crown study right after we married and summed it up this way: Debt is bad, saving is good, giving is fun, and stuff is meaningless. Angela suggested we begin each year with a planning session to set our business, personal, and couple goals together, keeping these principles in mind. I learned my lesson the first time around and wanted to do all I could to make sure I became a better husband and father.

MORE THAN BANKING

Today, Angela and I live on a farm and love the rural lifestyle. We enjoy getting our hands dirty with a large garden and an assortment of animals. Angela started raising goats and discovered that there are many uses for goat milk. She started experimenting with making goat milk soap and giving it to friends and family. That was the beginning of Kentucky Soaps and Such based on Main Street in Stanford, which now offers a wide variety of Kentucky products and gift baskets.

We began renovating run-down houses to be used as guesthouses for the many visitors that come through Stanford related to our companies and foundation. After deciding to open our guesthouses to the public, we realized we needed a place for people to eat downtown.

Around the same time, our son Preston started a sustainable farming operation called Marksbury Farm Market. They raise and process grass-finished cattle and pigs with no hormones or antibiotics. This gave us a great source for local proteins, so we decided to open a farm-to-table restaurant in Stanford called The Bluebird.

Both Angela and I have a passion for history and historic preservation, so bringing old buildings back to life, creating a vibrant local economy, and using all this for hospitality serve our business and community. Currently, our hospitality businesses include the Stanford Inn with eight rooms and six guesthouses, meeting rooms, catering, two restaurants, a wellness spa, and a gift shop.

Angela and I also love traveling to Italy. There, we became inspired by the "village" idea to bring back the stonework, landscaping, outdoor dining, and businesses that help keep life flowing vibrantly in a downtown. It inspires us to keep growing our local community.

Our banks are in thirteen communities around Kentucky. Most of the buildings we own were built in the 1800s or early 1900s, so we've spent a lot of money on renovating those. Our company invests in the community, not only by surrounding our banks with other high-quality businesses and preserving historic sites but also by ensuring our buildings are properly maintained, restored, and emblematic of our vision. We want our company and its surrounding area to represent something the community can be proud of. And I'm happy to say, I think we've come a long way in accomplishing that mission.

Banking is our main business, but around twenty-five years ago, we decided to acquire a life insurance company based in Springfield, Illinois. That deal worked out well for us, so we bought another insurance company from Houston, Texas. In recent years, we relocated the insurance company offices to Stanford.

A SPECIAL THANKS

Whenever I'm asked about influential people in my life, I always mention my mother and father first. They encouraged all of their kids to be entrepreneurial. My parents never *gave* us money. Rather, we were told that if we wanted something, we had to earn it. I'm forever grateful for that lesson, as I firmly believe that it greatly shaped my later success.

My parents were also charitable people. For most of my father's career, he gave away about half of his income.

Toward the end of his days on this earth, he tried to give away as much as possible.

I would be seriously remiss if I didn't mention what my dear brother Vince meant to me as well. He was a great brother, a longtime friend, and an amazing business partner who taught me more about the value of life and how to live it than anyone else.

My wife, Angela, who is my number one advisor and my best friend, makes our life a joy, whether or not we are in the high points or the low points of our lives. I am thankful to God for bringing me a great life partner. I am also thankful for our entire team at First Southern National Bank, UTG, and the River Foundation. I have been blessed to have many partners and team members who have been with me most of my career.

MY ADVICE

Another great influence in my life was my good friend and business partner Doug Ditto. Back in our college days, he once wisely told me, "Who you're with is much more important than what you do." In other words, it's all about the people around you. I've found truth in those words throughout my career.

I used to be a bit of a table pounder in meetings, ordering

people about what to do and when to do it. Then I noticed something: *the way you treat your team is the way they will treat your customers.*

We have been intentional about creating a culture in our businesses built on generosity. This means that we do lots of little things. For example, we like giving people monetary support if they are adopting a child. We give our team members time off to go on a short-term mission trip or do volunteer work in their community. Those things mean a lot to people, and I'm happy to be part of such a great team working together.

One final piece of advice I would give to any aspiring entrepreneur is to find someone you want to be like and go to work for them. Choose someone who embodies all the aspects of life you want to replicate. Go to work for them; see how they handle life and relationships. Find what it is you admire about them and try to infuse some of that in your own endeavors. For me, finding someone who is serious about their faith journey makes that an even richer experience.

"The way you treat your team is the way they will treat your customers."

JOE CRAFT

 Where Kentucky Boulevard and Parkway cross, there's a corner where my friends and I would sit and talk about whatever was going on in the world. I did that from as far back as I can remember all the way until I went to college. Once in a while, I will go back there to sit and reminisce about what a great place Hazard, Kentucky was to grow up. It has always been a place where honest, hardworking, and kindhearted people live, work, and contribute to the community. From my perspective, there's no better place for a kid with ambition and a dream to create a great life for himself and others than where I grew up. I am truly fortunate to have been brought up in such an environment.

Growing up, I had good role models telling me to get a good education and find a purpose for my passion for contributing to society. Local politicians used to come around and speak to the kids in Hazard all the time. And a few not-so-local politicians would show up once in a while too. For example, Bobby Kennedy came to Hazard in 1967 when I was in high school. In fact, there's a photo on the web page for Hazard County's history that shows him walking down the street, and even though I'm hidden, I was there.

I got a taste of what it was like to run a business working for my dad when I was about sixteen years old. My father and a neighbor owned The Pantry Shelf, which was a convenience store—the first of its kind in Hazard. They hired me to act as assistant manager, which meant that in the morning, I swept the driveway and opened the door for the manager to come in and run the store from eight in the morning until closing time. After closing, I went back, cleaned the floors, stocked the shelves, and locked the door until the next day. The convenience store business was new at the time, and it gave me the opportunity to see what it was like to build and run a business serving customers.

My immediate path after graduating from high school was clear. I needed to further my education so I could follow the words of wisdom from the positive influences in my life. With that at the forefront of my mind, I enrolled in the University of Kentucky (UK), where I initially received a bachelor of science in accounting in 1972 and got my juris doctorate (JD) in 1976.

I come from three generations of lawyers, so obtaining my JD seemed like an almost inevitable outcome. The accounting degree I got first, however, provided me with a well-rounded knowledge base to apply as a business leader. In fact, I got a job for an accounting firm while I was still studying as an undergraduate. It seemed like that would be integral to the career path I would choose. However, sometimes fate has a different idea about our individual journeys. The key is to understand when an opportunity is present.

WHEN CRISIS LEADS TO OPPORTUNITY

In the early 1970s, the oil crisis hit America. Anyone old enough to remember that time in history will recall the days of waiting in lines twenty cars deep for fuel at their local gas stations. The crisis had forced our government to seek alternative ways to harness energy, which led to a ramp-up of nuclear and coal plants. The infusion of capital into the coal industry was a Godsend to many areas of Kentucky, including Hazard. It created jobs and gave the hardworking citizens a chance to make a good life for themselves.

Like many Kentuckians, I was a beneficiary of the career opportunities created by the coal plants opening across the eastern United States. While attending UK, I received a phone call from a gentleman who was the Chief Executive Officer (CEO) of a coal-producing company in Eastern Kentucky. The company, Falcom Coal, was beginning to expand in response to the energy crisis, and he wanted me to work for them for the summer, which I did. That led to me getting a job offer when I graduated from law school. This ended up being a blessing because that job offer from the coal company paid great dividends going forward, as they offered me a permanent position and that started me on my entrepreneurial journey.

Falcon's goal was always to build the company to a certain level of profitability and sell it. I knew that from the time I was hired. Regardless, the job was a tremendous opportunity for me to get my foot in the door of a business within the coal industry, which had tremendous growth potential at the time.

In 1979, Falcon Coal was sold to Diamond Shamrock. During the sales process, I met folks from Tulsa, Oklahoma who worked for Mapco Inc., which was a pipeline company that wanted to invest in coal. Although they were not successful in buying Falcon, they were successful in convincing me to move to Tulsa in 1980 to work for them as general counsel for their coal company.

In 1982, I was promoted to general counsel for the parent company. In 1985, I was elected senior vice president of legal and finance. One year later, I became head of the coal division at Mapco. Ten years after that, working with the Beacon Group Private Equity Fund, I led a management buyout of the coal division. In 1999, we formed Alliance Resource Partners, LP, the first coal company master limited partnership (MLP) to be publicly traded and listed on the Nasdaq Stock Exchange. The Beacon fund exited its investment in Alliance Resource Partners, LP for around $150 million. In July 2022, the market cap for the partnership trades around $2.6 billion.

BECOMING A SERVANT LEADER

In 1992, I experienced another defining moment when I attended the Sloan School for Management at MIT. This is where I learned about a new leadership style that I still implement today. It's called servant leadership and the philosophy is largely about empowering workers—the people who know the job better than anyone—to make decisions and bring fresh ideas to the table.

Previously, the leadership style I know about was based on a command-and-control situation. At MIT, I learned how to use an inverted leadership model. Think about an organizational hierarchy as an inverted pyramid, where the workers are at the top and the leaders are at the bottom, serving the needs of the workers who are empowered with shared decision making. That style of leadership proved immensely successful, as I learned more by listening to the hardworking coal miners and other workers in our business than I ever did before.

Servant leadership provides fresh, purposeful ideas from a larger pool of people in the organization. The company isn't limited to the thoughts of executives; it gets involvement from all over the company. Thus, providing a spectrum of valuable insights leading to a significant competitive advantage.

As previously mentioned, Alliance Resource Partners went public in 1999, and I assumed the role of President and CEO. Over the years, my team and I have led the company to become the second largest coal producer in the eastern United States, with mining complexes in Illinois, Indiana, Kentucky, Maryland, Pennsylvania, and West Virginia. We sell primarily to electric utilities all over the country. Perhaps most importantly, we have created thousands of jobs for people in all those areas.

LEADING THE BUSINESS THROUGH ENERGY TRANSITION

Today, I find myself renewed because of the energy transition that's happening on a global scale. Currently, there are headwinds gaining strength to close down coal plants, so our company has spent the last six years determining how we can take our cash from the existing business to grow a sustainable future. With that in mind, we've come up with five verticals in which to allocate our free cash flow and focus our attention.

The first vertical we've identified is the distributions to our shareholders. We're still a MLP, so our shareholder base is focused on getting dividend distributions as a yield vehicle.

Our second is to continue to invest in our coal business. The only difference moving forward is that we'll ensure that the company becomes and remains a low-cost producer. The coal industry has been a critical contributor to the wealth of our nation for the past forty years, and we believe the coal industry should be a viable contributor to our country's domestic energy needs for decades to come.

The third vertical addresses the needs of our oil and gas business, which we began investing in around 2014. In 2022, that business will make a little over $100 million, and we will continue to reinvest the profits there.

Our fourth vertical concerns investments in growing businesses that can operate and be managed for the long term. One such investment is in a technology company called Matrix that we started in 2006. Initially focused on designing and implementing technology to support safety and efficiency for underground coal mining operations, Matrix is currently delivering products and services around the world focused on data networking, communication and tracking systems, industrial collision avoidance systems, and data analytics software. Included in these offerings is an advanced artificial intelligence-driven camera software for forklifts that is well positioned for meaningful growth.

The fifth vertical is targeting investments that are in the energy transition space. Industrial real estate will likely be a pivotal factor in this area, as it could lead to prosperous investments in recycling, solar power, carbon sequestration, water usage, and other battery storage-related areas. In 2022, Alliance invested in an electric vehicle charging station company and an innovative electric motor company that is focused on reducing carbon emissions compared to existing motors.

If we can properly execute our management of these five verticals, Alliance Resource Partners will continue to be immensely successful as the world undergoes energy transition.

Our success in navigating the transition of this industry will largely depend on finding great people with innovation in their skillset to pull the company forward. It's time for me to find those people that I can hire who will create products that the new world needs and values.

The company has plenty of resources for creative leaders

to build and grow businesses. Another key area of focus for me now is to find people who know how to leverage technology to come up with solutions that can build and grow a company the same way we did in 1999 when Alliance Resource Partners was founded. We can provide people with game-changing solutions with the financial resources they need. It's strange how exciting a time it is for me fifty years after my career began.

GIVING BACK WITH THE CRAFT ACADEMY

One of the greatest gifts bestowed on the American entrepreneur is the ability to give back to the community and serve the greater good. I am fortunate to be in a position where I can pledge the vast majority of my resources to the causes I care about most. One of those causes that is nearest and dearest to my heart is the Craft Academy, which is a two-year early college for exceptional students in their junior and senior years of high school.

As of 2022, the Craft Academy has had five graduating classes and has been ranked in the top twenty-five schools in the nation for STEM programs. Our students are some of the best in the nation, and they're getting opportunities to attend prestigious universities.

The Foundation for Appalachian Kentucky in Hazard helps me to provide GAP scholarships to graduates from the Craft

Academy. They have a panel that takes care of the screening process and makes all the selections. I am not involved in that personally, but I thank these wonderful people who enable my wife and I to finance college educations for young people who won't need to start their lives swimming in debt. The only requirement for a prospective student to apply is to be a resident of the state of Kentucky.

A SPECIAL THANKS

A prerequisite to being an entrepreneur involves caring about people. The only way I've seen people reach their dream is through constant teamwork. For me, my most special thanks go to the coal miners who have worked so hard for our company over the years. They are genuine heroes in my mind.

Whenever I need a boost, I go to the coal mine and see these American heroes in action. That reinvigorates me every time. All I need to do is talk to them and I can't help but soak in some of their tireless work ethic and inspiration.

Another special thanks goes to Brian Raney and the rest of the group at Awesome Inc for celebrating the accomplishments of entrepreneurs all over the great state of Kentucky. What they do is more than a recognition of business leaders; it's an observance of the American Spirit and gives everybody involved with the Kentucky Entrepreneur Hall of Fame a moment to understand the value of job creation.

MY ADVICE

Whenever a young entrepreneur approaches me for an answer about how to start a business, I always ask a series of questions: "What's your idea? What's the market? What is the demand that you think needs to be met? Do you understand the business model? Is there already a business implementing something similar, or are you attempting to disrupt the industry? You must have the answers to those questions before starting any new business.

The next thing I tell them is to work for someone who understands how your business model works. Learn from them. Find out everything you can about how other people in similar businesses make decisions. Without that, you'll start from scratch, which means you won't be prepared for certain inevitabilities of that industry. You'll also try things that you think are new and innovative but other people have already tried to no avail. That will set you back.

If you don't learn the business firsthand from others who have already seen what works and what doesn't, you'll make things much harder on yourself. Take a year or two to work in the industry. Start with a small business because you'll get the most experience there. Large businesses won't give you the exposure you'll need about how everything works. *The entrepreneurial path is not meant to be a get-rich-quick scheme; it is something to be played for the long game.* Be smart, work hard, plan for the future, and enjoy the ride.

"The entrepreneurial path is not meant to be a get-rich-quick scheme; it is something to be played for the long game."

JIM HEADLEE

 I grew up in Evansville, Indiana. My mother and father were wonderful people with solid values and set a good example for me, my older sister, and my two younger brothers. Mom and Dad attended the University of Evansville and stressed the value of a good education.

Following in their footsteps, I also chose to attend the University of Evansville, where I obtained my degree in business. As it turned out, my choice for college proved highly beneficial. Not only did I get a solid education, but I also met my wife, Jenny. We have been married forty-four years with four grown children and seven grandchildren.

Fresh out of college, I decided to work in the oil and gas leasing business. I was a landman and my role was to secure drilling rights for oil and gas exploration companies.

My first stint in that sector was working in mineral and land management for the oil company Conoco. I then took that first step into the entrepreneurial track and became an equity owner in two mineral leasing businesses.

When oil prices dropped to only $10 per barrel, I realized oil exploration would drastically reduce and so would my business. Natural gas was beginning to deregulate, so I took a sales position with EnTrade and moved to their headquarters in Louisville, Kentucky. This eventually led to the role of national sales manager for the natural gas marketer EnTrade Corporation.

During the next five years, the company grew from 25 to 125 employees and nearly $500 million in annual revenue. Unfortunately (depending on how you look at it), all did not end well for me in that company. As is the case with most things in life, a brightly shining silver lining was on the horizon, as my departure from EnTrade ended up being just the thing to kick-start my entrepreneurial journey.

PUT YOUR FAITH IN INTEGRITY EVERY TIME

The beginning of the end for me at EnTrade happened

when I got a call from one of our good customers at Georgia Pacific. He told me, "We're not happy with what's going on at your company. I tried to talk with your salesperson, but he keeps blowing us off. You overcharged us, and I need someone to admit it and do something about it."

I said, "Okay, let me look into this and get back to you."

After a little more than a cursory investigation, it became clear to me that the customer was right; one of our sales reps had intentionally not lowered the gas price for several months at their Michigan plant hoping it would go unnoticed. In my view, we clearly owed them a refund and an apology. Our new Chief Operating Officer (COO) didn't see it that way when I informed him of the situation. He did not want to admit to the overcharge or offer a refund. I told him, "The only way I know to handle this is to apologize and pay back the overage. And if you want to handle it any other way, you'll have to do it yourself." I made the mistake to be so absolute with him. He didn't like me questioning his judgment so strongly.

Two weeks later, I was called into the President's office on a Monday morning. There sat the COO. I knew what was going on as soon as I walked in the door. They were firing me. It would have been easy for me to tell them what I thought and give them a piece of my mind, but I did none of those things. Instead, I listened to what they had to say (even though I intensely disagreed), stood up, shook hands, and walked out of the room.

When I walked back to my office, a contracted outplacement person was waiting for me. They watched me take five minutes to load up my personal belongings and escort me out the door, marking my last day with EnTrade. When I crossed that threshold from the building to the parking lot, I couldn't help but feel like God's voice was telling me, "You did the right thing, Jim, and you're going to be fine because of it." It was a dark moment, but little did I realize that God was writing the next chapter of my story, which would be part of something bigger he was writing for hundreds of people who would join me in a business I had not yet thought of—Summit Energy.

REACHING THE SUMMIT

An aha moment is supposed to occur in our darkest of times. Now comes the part in my story when I'm supposed to explain how everything came together all at once. Well, that's not exactly how it happened for me.

My entrepreneurial success started with nothing more than an idea that would allow me a way to pay our family living expenses in the short term. I never expected the idea to turn into a business procuring and managing the natural gas and electricity for 17,000 sites worldwide in sixty countries managing $20 billion in annual energy expenditures for hundreds of Fortune 1,000 clients, but it did.

It was December 1991 when Summit Energy was born from the basement of my home. The idea was simple enough: I thought, "Buying energy is complex for most businesses—too complex to keep up with and understand for even a corporation spending millions per year on their natural gas and electricity to run their multiple plants in multiple states. Could they delegate to someone else on their staff? Sure, but they're not going to know much about it either. Natural gas has been deregulated and the same thing will happen with electricity soon. Customers don't have anywhere to go for answers. They don't know when they're paying too much or what their options are. But I do. I know about all the complexities; I also know about how to get the best deals done."

Then I made phone calls—lots of them. I always tried to instill a sense of trust with whomever I spoke to. I told each person, "If you hire us, we will do what we say we'll do. We will prove ourselves worthy of your trust."

When Summit Energy was in its early stages, outsourcing wasn't as common as it is today. Some people were receptive to the idea, but others were more cautious. One client said, "I understand your value. You know more about oil and gas than I ever will. How about I pay you $500 per month and I can call you anytime for advice?" It seemed like I would be on a retainer of sorts. With nowhere else to go, it seemed like a fair enough option, so I agreed to his suggestion.

Several years later, we were now fully managing their natural gas and electricity spend for all their plants in the United States, China, and elsewhere around the world. I was even invited to one of their annual conferences to be recognized as one of their key partners. I couldn't help but think how strange it was that we went from a $500-per-month consultant to managing the entire energy spend for this global corporation.

This was just the beginning for Summit Energy, my entrepreneurial journey, and my understanding of leadership.

LEARNING TO LEAD

In the early days of Summit Energy, I was focused almost entirely on bringing new business in the door. When the company grew to about fifty employees, I began to realize that I had no idea how to provide leadership. One team member asked me about feedback and another asked me about vision. I couldn't supply either of them with sufficient answers, so I dedicated my focus on learning how to become a better leader.

I met with several people in leadership positions and picked up a book called *The Leadership Challenge* by James Kouzes and Barry Posner. They interviewed thousands of people and came up with the top five practices of exemplary leadership. This theory has since become a widely recognized and highly lauded approach. I'll always be grateful for that knowledge.

According to the authors, the most important practice of exemplary leadership by far is to "encourage the heart of those you lead." This means actively seeking to bring out the best in people. Show appreciation for a job well done. Thank them, and do it often. It builds high morale and affirms your people. Let them know you value their thoughts and ideas.

This leadership lesson became especially valuable when Summit Energy purchased another company in Europe called GFE. Summit had about 220 employees at the time and GFE had about 80. I wanted those eighty employees in our newly acquired company to feel welcomed and part of the team. Someone in my marketing department suggested I write a personalized, handwritten letter to each of them. This was something we made a habit of doing quite often with our own employees on their work anniversary. It sounded like a good idea to extend a welcoming gesture, so that was the focus of my leadership for the next two weeks.

Over that period of time, I wrote each one of the GFE employees a personal letter mentioning how we were pleased they were part of GFE (now Summit Energy) and thanked them for their role in the combined company. We were counting on them to help make us the best company in the world at managing energy. I also mentioned that I looked forward to meeting them on my next trip to their homeland. I included some notepads and pens with GFE and Summit branding on them and hoped they would feel like an important part of the team.

Not long after I sent those letters, my inbox became flooded with wonderful responses. People were incredibly appreciative of the personal note to thank them, and just about all of them told me how I could count on them to help us be the best in the industry. This was a powerful lesson for me in supporting that key leadership lesson provided by Kouzes and Posner to "encourage the heart."

INTEGRITY COMES FULL CIRCLE

Ironically, twelve years after the formation of Summit Energy, I had an opportunity to make a presentation to try to win the business of a familiar company—Georgia Pacific. This is the same company I took a stand for when working at EnTrade (and you know how that turned out).

The meeting took place in one of Georgia Pacific's conference rooms on the thirty-sixth floor of their building on Peachtree Boulevard in Atlanta. I was seated at one end of the table and the senior Georgia Pacific person was seated at the other end. Ten other Georgia Pacific representatives with various stakes in the game sat on each side of the table.

I started my presentation about why Summit Energy could effectively represent Georgia Pacific in its energy management solutions for the future. After a few minutes, the company's president asked me, "Jim, how is it that you started Summit Energy?"

I thought, "Do I even go there?" Without too much hesitation, I decided honesty is just about always the best policy, so I told him, "Well, I used to work for a gas marketing and supply company called EnTrade that supplied natural gas for your Michigan plant. There was a discrepancy in the price. I took a stand for integrity, sided with Georgia Pacific, and lost my job for it. So I started this energy management company and I'm glad I did."

One person spoke up and said, "I remember that issue with EnTrade."

We didn't speak any more about the situation until I finished my presentation. At that point, the corporate person who remembered the deal caught me in the hallway and said, "I'm a longtime consultant for Georgia Pacific. In fact, they're 25 percent of my income, but I'm recommending they hire you and diminish my services because you have a more complete service offering. Besides that, you stood up for *integrity* over money. Way to go!"

I was nearly speechless. All I could do was shake his hand, smile, and thank him for his sentiment. We walked out of the building that day and got a phone call not long after, telling us that Summit Energy was awarded the business. I still can't believe how that happened. God blessed us with that deal, and I've never forgotten it. Stand up for what's right and you never know when things will come full circle for you.

TEACH TO TRANSFORM

In 2008, I wanted to sell Summit Energy, but I also wanted to make sure it was in good hands. Thirty-nine companies put in a bid to purchase the business. We narrowed the field to eleven and eventually chose a private equity company in Boston. They were the best fit for our employees and management.

After selling Summit Energy, Jenny and I had the opportunity to use our foundation to help others who were serving people in need. We were pleased to be able to join Dr. Tom McKechnie to begin a charitable foundation called Teach to Transform. This ministry collaborates with partners who are serving impoverished countries around the world with the least medical resources and darkest spiritual needs. Tom is an ER doctor who travels with his teams across the world teaching those who can teach others long after Tom and his teams have left.

A SPECIAL THANKS

Forget about all those hardball negotiation tactics. I realized that great deals are done when a salesperson can become a trusted advisor to create a win-win situation.

As my career progressed, I was fortunate to gain valuable insight from another gentleman named Gregg Dedrick. He and I knew each other because we went to the same church. Every Monday morning, we would meet for coffee. I always brought a journal with me because he had so many great ideas. Gregg told me that a lot of them came from his boss, David Novak. All I knew was that when Gregg spoke, I listened intently because almost everything he said made so much sense and provided a unique perspective I had not considered. I also wrote his thoughts down so I could remember them and translate their intended meaning more clearly for my own leadership. Gregg was always available to brainstorm or think through issues with me. I am a better leader today for having met him, and I'm proud to say we're still very good friends.

MY ADVICE

Travel light. That's the best advice I can give any person. If there is something or someone weighing you down, work yourself up to forgive them and move on. Let it go.

When I left EnTrade, I was angry. At first, I carried that anger around with me, but I realized I needed to do something about being a victim. With this negative mindset, I was not being the kind of husband or father my family needed me to be. It was all due to this baggage I was carrying with me everywhere I went. Then I thought about God. I said, "Well, if He can forgive me, I guess I can forgive those people from my past employer."

With forgiveness as my purpose, I wrote a note to the President of that company. It said something like, "I feel like I performed well while working for your company, and I wanted to let you know that I'm sorry about what happened. I still don't feel like it's right, but life is too short to dwell on the situation. You still owe me severance, but I want you to consider that debt forgiven."

Once I put that letter in the mailbox, I felt this massive burden being lifted off my shoulders. Sending that letter of forgiveness freed me up to move on. There is liberation in forgiveness. Wow! I was traveling lighter and it felt good! This cleared my mind for much more mental space to create and innovate an opportunity for positive change! I learned that Christ provides all of us with a way out; we just have to accept it and move on.

From time to time, I stop and ponder if there is something weighing me down. In the quietness of my soul I ask, do I feel the need to forgive or resolve something with somebody? If so, I do it and feel the renewed energy fill my headspace. Travel light!

> "From time to time, I stop and ponder if there is something weighing me down. In the quietness of my soul I ask, do I feel the need to forgive or resolve something with somebody? If so, I do it and feel the renewed energy fill my headspace. Travel light!"

PART 5

2019 INDUCTEES: MICHAEL DAVIS, NATE MORRIS, DEBBIE SCOPPECHIO, AND R. D. WEBB

MICHAEL DAVIS

Although I've never really thought of myself as an entrepreneur, I guess the writing was on the wall as far back as fifth grade. That's when I began renting comic books with a friend of mine. I like to think we were the Netflix of its day. Unfortunately, we got in a fair amount of trouble when the school discovered what we were doing. Before that, however, we made a fair amount of money for a couple of elementary school kids.

Besides comic books, I developed a strong interest in science and business early in life. During my senior year of high school, I added technology to that list of things that piqued my curiosity. The Apple II computer caught my attention that year and I became fascinated with writing code and working in the computer lab.

From my fifth-grade side hustle to my passion for technology in high school, I eventually found my way to the University of Louisville (UofL), where I enhanced my aptitude for technology.

THANKS BUT NO THANKS

One of my professors at UofL worked at a small company that designed computer systems for large office buildings. He came to class one day and asked if anyone would be interested in a co-op job. I jumped at the chance because I wanted to see the real-world applications of what we studied at school. Fortunately, he granted me the opportunity and brought me on board to help that company set up automated systems to run their accounting software.

That position was my first full-time job and my career accelerated alongside the rapid company growth. Things went pretty well there for several years, until a fateful afternoon when I pitched an idea to my boss. He said, "Okay, but just don't spend any company time on it." I agreed and made one small and easy enough request to grant. "Just give me half of whatever you sell it for when it's done," I said. Although that meeting didn't exactly leave me feeling inspired, I remained undeterred in my mission to create something meaningful.

For the next several months, I spent nights and weekends writing software. I stayed true to my word to not work on the idea during my regular hours. When the finished product was ready, I presented it to the company. Everybody thought it was an excellent solution and complimented me for my innovation. The company then sold the software, which I created with my own "free time," to Sears for about $40,000. Surely, this would put me on the fast track to success in that company, right? Not exactly.

Later that year, the company held a Christmas party. A part of the festivities was an award ceremony to recognize employees who performed especially well or contributed in an extraordinary way during the year. I didn't care much about gaining any special recognition. All I wanted was for them to hold their end of the bargain; I wanted half of what they sold my innovation for.

Toward the end of the ceremony, they called me up on stage, which I sort of expected to happen. They presented me with a plaque for the contribution of my software. "That's nice," I thought, as I smiled and was happy to join in the celebration. Taped to the back of the plaque, I found an envelope that said "Thank you" on the front. Inside the envelope was a check for $1,000.

That was about $19,000 short of the mark. I immediately walked over to my boss and told him, "I quit."

That was the moment my entrepreneurial spirit officially took flight.

THE PEOPLE YOU MEET MAKE THE BIGGEST DIFFERENCE

The silver lining in my several years working for that company was the people I met. In particular, I established a relationship with one of the most brilliant people I've ever known—Yung Nguyen. Yung was a genius innovator at writing software. Whereas most of the people who worked for that company had backgrounds that included some form of privilege, Yung had quite a different experience. He was a Vietnamese refugee and heroically escaped the country to flee the Communist government. As a twenty-year-old immigrant, he fought his way out of oppression in his country and began working locally in restaurants to save up enough money to attend the UofL.

Yung knew very little English in his first few years in the United States. What he lacked in language, he made up for with brilliant engineering. While working at the same company, Yung and I quickly became close friends and began thinking about how we could start our own business.

TRAGEDY STRIKES

Around the same time that Yung and I were brainstorming, a sad and horrifying event occurred.

A young woman by the name of Mary Byron had been stalked and raped by her ex-boyfriend. The offender was justly put in prison for the crime. While awaiting trial, however, someone had posted bail for him. Just before regaining his temporary freedom, this individual vowed to kill Mary. Shortly after his release, this disturbed criminal seized his opportunity on his unknowing victim.

On December 6, 1993 (the night of her twenty-first birthday), Mary Byron had just completed her shift in a store at a local shopping mall. It was a cold night, so when she got into the car, Mary started the engine and waited a few minutes to get warm. While waiting, her attacker approached the car from the driver's side and shot and murdered Mary at point-blank range. Mary's life was taken from her because nobody knew that a violent criminal, with a senseless personal vendetta against her, was loose.

The next morning, her parents, John and Pat Byron, appeared on the local news and told reporters that if they knew her ex-boyfriend was out of jail, they would have taken their daughter far out of harm's way. The reason their daughter was brutally murdered was because the technology didn't yet exist to alert people to the status of potentially dangerous criminals. The idea of stopping tragedies, like the one that happened to Mary Byron, became the genesis of what Yung and I wanted to form a company around. We knew the technology was available and we knew we could make it work if we were given the chance.

NECESSITY BECOMES THE MOTHER OF INVENTION AGAIN

For some time, Yung and I had been researching ideas about how a computer and a phone system could open up access to information. It became clear to us instantly that Mary's murder might have been prevented if the information in the jail's computer was easily accessible by phone.

Shortly after the tragedy of Mary Byron, I called the county judge's office and asked if anyone was working on the issue that ultimately led to her killing. I found out that a small group of people were already looking into what could be done. We connected with those folks and began the process of visioning an automated system to let people know who was in jail and who was recently released.

The county then put out a request for proposal (RFP) for someone to attempt to solve the problem about six months later. Huge telecom companies like MCI and AT&T put together bids. So did a little-known company called Interactive Systems, which was basically Yung and me.

By calling around to see what the county was looking at, we knew that the county didn't have a lot of money to spend on this project. The big telcos were suggesting solutions that would have cost hundreds of thousands of dollars. Yung and I bid $60,000, which gave us a big advantage.

We hadn't heard anything about the bidding process for a long time, until one day when Yung and I had just finished getting my car washed. The radio was on, and we thought we heard the news announce Interactive Systems as the winning bidder to build a victim notification service. We were shocked but still uncertain of what we just heard. Sure enough, the people in charge of awarding the bid called us later that day to say that we had won the contract.

At first, it was tough for us to believe that we went up against those giants of industry and came out on top. We didn't even have an office. Our plan was to put our system together in a basement. After taking a few minutes to celebrate and catch our breath, Yung and I quickly got to work. From there, we were off to the races.

VINE GOES ONLINE

After six months of toiling in Yung's basement, we installed a computer in the basement of Jefferson County Jail and designed an interface to pull the data we needed from their computer. After weeks of testing, we were done; that was our first system. One year after Mary's death, we unveiled the nation's first automated victim notification service. It became known as VINE (Victim Information and Notification Everyday).

When VINE first went online, it blew up...not literally. Almost as soon as it went live, twenty-four phone lines ran solid busy for several weeks. More people than we even imagined used our service as a way to alert people of potentially dangerous individuals being at large.

Over the next several months, we had no choice but to expand the system exponentially. The demand was unbelievable, as cities all over the country were talking about it. Immediately, we got calls from investors who wanted to have a stake in our innovation. We were more than happy to take on venture capital because we had no money and needed to leave our day jobs.

Within a month or so, we had a deal struck with David Jones Jr. and Doug Cobb from Chrysalis Ventures in Louisville to invest in our business. This allowed us to quit our day jobs and focus full time on our business. The problem our company addressed was happening all over America, so we rapidly expanded to capture this brand-new market.

THE EVOLUTION OF A BUSINESS

Interactive Systems was later renamed Appriss, Inc., as our service offerings expanded. About 95 percent of the country is now served by our original VINE program. Appriss manages the jails and prisons all over America to let victims know when offenders are out of custody or when they have an upcoming court date.

With the growth of our victim notification service came the expansion of the company. VINE now accounts for only about 20 percent of the company's business today. We spent about ten years building our network and gathered so much data about people going through the criminal justice system that we began building adjacent products.

Five years after we launched VINE, we began building a suite of products that leveraged our data to assist law enforcement in solving problems related to criminal justice.

In the mid-2000s, methamphetamine was a big problem in the United States. Appriss built a network that would track people who were buying cold medicine in bulk. Cold medicine is a key ingredient in cooking methamphetamine.

With our data, we now work with 95 percent of the pharmacy-industry retailers around the country. Over a ten-year period, we drove the domestic meth lab production down by 85 percent.

Unfortunately, the drug problem in America has evolved, but we have attempted to evolve with it. With domestic meth labs having their capacity diminished extensively, drug trafficking in America has shifted to opioid abuse.

Appriss now monitors about 90 percent of opioid prescriptions nationally. The success of those last two products has given us access to retail customers like Walmart, CVS, Walgreens, and others. Now we also help those companies solve fraud problems. This rounds out the trio of our markets that comprise our "Knowledge for Good" business model:

1. Public safety through the victim notification service.
2. Battling substance abuse disorders by tracking methamphetamine and opioid usage.
3. Fighting retail fraud by identifying customers and employees attempting to commit fraud.

We've since sold the public safety sector of our business to Equifax for a little over $1.8 billion. The other two sectors are still thriving under Appriss's ownership. It's also worth mentioning that Appriss has never focused on advertising strategies or political influence. That's why we're probably the most unknown big-data company on the planet.

TIMING AND LUCK PLAY A ROLE IN EVERY SUCCESS STORY

Being smart and working your tail off are table stakes for success in a new business. The thing you can't control is luck, and there is not a single story of success in the world where luck didn't play a role. Countless brilliant and hardworking people could have changed the world if they just caught a break or two. Every major success has a story to tell that includes a pivotal moment. If that pivotal moment didn't break just right, you probably would never have heard of Apple, Google, or whatever uber-successful company you can think of.

Our luck at Appriss came in the form of good timing. We started in 1994, about a month after the OJ Simpson trial began. It was on the air—virtually nonstop—for the next nine months. The situation brought domestic violence and victims of dangerous offenders to center stage for everyone with a television set to see. The trial triggered dozens of state-level mandates requiring victims of violent crimes to be notified when their offender is free from captivity.

Timing is everything. If our product was launched five years before that event, I'm not sure Appriss ever happens. We would have been too soon. If our product launched five years later, we almost certainly would have been too late. Another smart, hardworking team would have already served the need. See what I mean? Being smart and hardworking are table stakes traits of entrepreneurship. You will need to have timing and a little luck on your side as well.

Everything has to break just right, but if you keep trying,

working, and innovating, timing and luck will eventually collide with your efforts to change the world.

A SPECIAL THANKS

Nobody gets a company as far as Appriss has gone without being surrounded by elite talent. Over the years, I've been truly blessed to work with an abundance of super-intelligent people. Many of them are still driving the mission at Appriss today. I feel fortunate to have played the role I did as part of a big, brilliant team for many years.

There are several individuals to whom I owe a great deal of gratitude. For example, just about everything David Jones, Sr., founder of Humana, said to me was gold. One of the most impactful things he told me was, "You must be ready to reinvent your company; you can't keep doing the same thing." He shared how Humana had to do this throughout their history.

Knowing when it's time to pivot is critical to growth. The key word is pivot. You're not walking in a completely different direction. For example, Appriss started in the public safety sector; we pivoted to tracking substance abuse and preventing retail fraud. Those newer business sectors were side steps; the industries were related—adjacent, if you prefer. It's much easier to reinvent within similar categories than it is to break into an entirely different area of business.

David Jones, Sr. was a treasure to spend time with. He was a legend in Louisville and yet he took the time to come to our company's early Christmas parties. Although we made a lot of money for Chrysalis Ventures, that's not why he was there. It was his passion for helping young entrepreneurs that made him want to come and show his support. We lost a Louisville treasure when he passed.

Doug Cobb was also highly influential in our success. In the early days, he was a vital board member. Yung and I could take the company only so far. Eventually, Appriss arrived at an inevitable fork in the road. We could either keep the company small by staying only in the victim notification sector, or we could swing for the fences by branching out. That's when we asked Doug Cobb to join us as our CEO.

With Doug at the helm, I focused on product and Yung went to work on technology. That was when we transitioned from a startup to a business with management teams and the ability to scale. During a ten-year period, Doug taught me so many things before I needed to step back into the CEO role again in 2009.

David Jones, Sr. and Doug Cobb were both tremendously influential in my entrepreneurial journey and achieving success beyond anything I ever envisioned, even as an elementary school comic book-renting mogul. My biggest mentor, however, has always been Yung Nguyen. Although

Yung was only active with the company for its first six years, we've remained close friends since its inception. It's safe to say that Appriss would never be where it is today without him.

Yung is an inspiration to anyone faced with challenges. I used to sit across a boardroom table from him obsessively worrying about every little thing. Looking across the table, I would see Yung and remember his journey to escape Vietnam, immigrating to this great country of ours, fighting his way through school, and thinking and outworking everybody around him to become an amazing emblem of success. He would tell me about walking through Cambodia and Thailand while evading the authorities. In comparison, whatever I was worrying about was always nothing. Yung kept me centered; he was the guy I needed to balance some of my impulsivity. He was always so cool and unbelievably talented. We made a great team during the startup phase of our company.

MY ADVICE

I've already talked a lot about how being smart and working hard are prerequisites to entrepreneurship. Timing and luck will always play a role, but beyond that, you also need to be willing to trust those around you and give up control at the right point in your business.

A lot of young entrepreneurs I've spoken with are reluctant to give up control. *So many people think that business is all about negotiation. It's more about knowing when to give up a little control for an appropriate amount of capital.* That capital could be in the form of finances or knowledge. If you can get the right person on board or an influx of cash when needed, don't be afraid to let go of a small portion of the control. I could never have taken Appriss to where it is today without knowing who to bring in and when to seek investment. Be smart, work hard, and let go of control when the timing seems right. From there, all you need is timing and just a little luck. If all that happens, I just might be reading about your story in a future volume of this same book.

"So many people think that business is all about negotiation. It's more about knowing when to give up a little control for an appropriate amount of capital."

NATE MORRIS

With deep ties to Morgan County, I am proud to be a ninth-generation Kentuckian who comes from a long line of farmers and factory workers. My family history and journey are central to understanding my identity, as so much of who I am and what I aspire to achieve began right here in the Commonwealth.

My parents met while attending the University of Kentucky (UK) but parted ways when I was still quite young. This, of course, would have ramifications for my entire family. My mother had to raise me as a single, working parent, and I had to look elsewhere for fatherly guidance.

I once heard someone say, "Our fathers make us or break

us." Without even realizing it, my dad influenced my life through his absence. The fact that he did not pay child support, which he would later be arrested for, and other challenges compelled me to assume total responsibility for my own life.

Fortunately, my maternal grandparents were highly involved in my childhood and were a support system for my mom. They helped positively shape who I would become as an adult and had an encouraging and stabilizing effect on me. I learned so much through spending time with them and hearing their life stories and advice. That fatherly guidance that my dad never provided came mostly from my grandfather, Lewis Sexton. In fact, some of the most powerful lessons I ever learned about life and leadership came from him.

My grandfather was a good, hardworking man. He grew up on a farm but had the opportunity to work at the Ford auto assembly plant in Louisville. The opportunity was a janitor position at the plant, and it was his foot in the door to get other higher-paying jobs on the assembly line. He sprung at the job offer and moved his family to South Louisville, where I would later spend my formative years. My grandfather worked his way up at the auto plant and became so well respected that he was elected as the United Auto Workers Local 862 President. He became heavily involved in guiding his fellow workers to fair working conditions and negotiated incomes that could provide a better way of life for their families. I quickly learned from my grandfather that being a union leader had a lot to do with building community and problem solving, as does being a business leader.

Most of my relatives were proud auto workers. Like my grandfather, they all made cars for the two Ford Motor Company plants in town. That is why "Buy American" was a religion in our household. We bought American-made products to support American workers and their families in American companies, and we firmly believed, as I do today, that America was stronger for it.

In addition to my nineteen family members working in the factory, the other union members became an extension of my family. They taught me a lot about how to treat others. My grandfather used to always say, "You know, unions wouldn't need to exist if companies just did the right thing and took care of their people." Those words in particular have heavily influenced my entrepreneurial journey. They are a big reason why my company, Rubicon, pays 100 percent of the cost for quality healthcare for its workers. We are also proud to contribute many other benefits in exchange for our employees' skills, loyalty, strong work ethic, and shared vision to make a difference in the world. We have been certified by the global authority on workplace culture Great Place to Work® for five years in a row. The award is a recognition of Rubicon as having some of the best leadership in corporate culture in America.

EARLY LEADERSHIP EXPERIENCES

Ever since I was young, I have been driven to do something big. I was inspired by my grandfather as a leader and my single mother who worked and led her family. Their influence drove me to take on any problem that needs a solution, regardless of the challenge.

From elementary school to high school, I was involved with student government. I was student body president in grade school and president for my senior year of high school. Getting involved with student government helped me to understand a lot about working with others, driving results, and becoming a leader. Throughout school, I pursued all leadership opportunities.

One experience that was particularly impactful on my career was the American Legion Boys Nation. The American Legion is a group that enhances the well-being of America's veterans and their families. Each year, a select group of high school students was chosen for the program, and if selected, we had the opportunity to travel to Washington, DC to meet policymakers, elected officials, and even the President of the United States. At the time of my trip, President Bill Clinton was in office. This was unique because he attended the same program while growing up in Arkansas.

The opportunity to meet a sitting President and travel to

DC was an honor and an experience that would later drive my interest in government leadership. That experience also filled me with confidence. Knowing that a President of the United States had attended Boys Nation when he was my age made me feel like I could accomplish anything and it helped me to realize that anything was possible. I could go from being a working-class kid with an absent dad, similar to President Clinton's upbringing, to the most powerful man in the world. Boys Nation empowered me to build my own future, and I am forever grateful for my experience in this prestigious program.

In addition to my early leadership pursuits, I had other youthful interests. For example, I always loved football. I played throughout my school career, but an injury while playing in high school halted my plan of getting a football scholarship. That was a painful experience, and it forced me to find another way to pay for college. During my recovery, I watched the news 24/7, taking an interest in the political correspondents and their commentary. I threw myself into student government and my studies. As a result, I earned an ancient and accepted Scottish rite, a Freemasonry scholarship to attend George Washington University.

INVALUABLE POLITICAL EXPERIENCE

I worked in politics from the moment I set foot on George Washington's campus. In my freshman year, I worked for a member of the US House of Representatives named Anne Northup. Working for Representative Northup was a big break for me. She had a strong relationship with the future President, George W. Bush, and she would later introduce me to Senator Mitch McConnell's office. I interned for both Senator McConnell and his wife, Secretary Elaine Chao, while she was serving as Secretary of the US Department of Labor. By my junior year, I worked my way to an internship at the White House.

Throughout my various political roles in college, I gained invaluable experience. I learned how the government functioned at the highest levels—both the great successes and the great dysfunction. Nonetheless, observing and interacting with members of Congress, senators, and occasionally the President of the United States and their teams provided me with lessons in leadership I could never have received anywhere else. Perhaps most importantly, I learned that as a leader, particularly in an industry like waste management and recycling, one needs to understand the stifling role that regulations often play in business. Often, those regulations are lobbied for by the entrenched and powerful legacy companies to prevent competition and innovation from small startups. This is true in the waste industry among others and can stand in the way of new opportunities for small business owners.

Government should provide every incentive for entrepreneurs to take risks. Even though I had a distaste for government inefficiencies and waste in addition to the far-reaching regulations as a business leader, I knew it was critical to be in tune with current policies in Washington, DC and how they impact the business community.

FORESHADOWING CHINA'S THREAT TO AMERICA

During my involvement in the political arena, I became particularly interested and skilled in raising capital for politicians, which I found to be a transferable skill to my business career. I did not have any personal wealth of my own, but I got great advice from Mike Duncan. Mike was the Treasurer and General Counsel at the Republican National Committee (RNC), as well as a fellow Kentuckian. He told me, "If you want to accelerate your political trajectory, learn how to raise money. That is where you have a chance to get noticed quickly and move up the ranks."

I took Mike's words to heart and became especially skilled at raising money. At twenty-three, I received accolades for my ability to raise funds on the national level at such a young age for President George W. Bush's re-election campaign in 2004.

Shortly after Bush completed his second successful run for President, I worked at the American Red Cross. While serving there, I followed Hurricane Katrina, which was a crash course for me in disaster management and how to respond to some of the toughest crises that can impact leaders at all levels.

The American Red Cross also provided me with an opportunity to work in China where I taught at a university and worked for the Kentucky Cabinet for Economic Development. It was evident at the time that China was a rising economic superpower that could someday challenge America.

As a leader, I knew I would be dealing with China in some way for the rest of my life. China had grown consistently and was poised to become the biggest threat to America's global dominance. Back in the early 2000s, when China was first admitted into the World Trade Organization, it was clear to all who were paying attention that the country would be a force that could not be ignored in a few decades. With 1.3 billion people, if China could go from being very poor to middle class, it would mean a great opportunity to sell American products overseas or, if things went badly, a major threat to our prosperity.

One of my first inclinations of China's potential prominence in the global economy was how the country affected Kentucky. First, I realized we were exporting a significant amount of bourbon to China. Then I realized that KFCs outnumbered McDonald's by a scale of three to one in the

Chinese mainland. It hit me, "If I want to be a leader for America, I need to understand what's happening in China going forward and what America needs to do to remain number one."

Teaching students about the American way of life and how we do business was an eye-opening experience. One of the tools I used to teach the Chinese students about American business was biography. Being a Kentuckian and with the popularity of KFC in China, I went with Colonel Sanders as a good example. After telling the story of how Harland Sanders (aka The Colonel) went from selling fried chicken at his roadside restaurant in Corbin, Kentucky to creating a global franchise phenomenon, one of the students asked me, "So how did the government influence the creation of KFC?" I replied, "That's the beauty of our system. The government wasn't involved. In America, you are encouraged to take risks and allowed to fail, without intervention from the government."

AMERICA'S RELATIONSHIP WITH GARBAGE: CROSSING THE RUBICON

Shortly after my time in China, I returned home and attended graduate school at Princeton. During my studies there, I came to an unsettling conclusion that our government was getting into the business of picking winners and losers on the environment.

Kentucky was pigeon-holed as a coal-producing state, and I felt like Washington, DC was unjustly picking on our amazing Commonwealth for one of its signature industries. That bothered me, so I set out to do something about it. I started brainstorming about ways to improve Kentucky's positioning in the eyes of the world, related to the environment. I thought, "There must be an environmental issue on which everybody can agree." I had been friends with Marc Spiegel since we were about fourteen years old. His family was in the waste business, so we connected the dots and thought about the trash industry as a pain point the entire country had in common.

Marc told me about the numerous inadequacies that were a signature hallmark of the industry at that time, so I started to investigate how the industry worked. The most shocking truth I unveiled was that the biggest waste management services made most of their money from landfills.

The big players in waste management are not trucking or transportation businesses, like a lot of people assume. By utilizing and profiting heavily on the landfill model, they are real estate companies. Their profit comes from picking up your garbage and dumping it into the landfill that they own. The fee they charge to take your garbage away is basically rent for storing it on their site. In essence, they are getting paid to create pollution and have no financial incentives to recycle anything.

That idea that Americans were paying people to fill up a massive hole in the ground instead of extracting valuable commodities by repurposing the garbage seemed insane. When you consider that the average person throws away at least six items per day, garbage is a universal problem. We all have it, but we all need to do something better about it. That was the foundational thought with which Rubicon was founded.

"How long can we continue to bury garbage in the ground?" I wondered. Society, at some point, will push back.

The other major problem I uncovered was the level of technology, or lack thereof, in the waste industry. Most of the major companies used little technology in both their operations and their collections. We set out to reimagine the entire waste category.

Rubicon was founded in 2008 and legally formed in 2009 here in Kentucky. I assumed more than our fair share of risk when starting the company by maxing out personal credit cards with a $10,000 limit to fund the early expenses of establishing the business. Fortune favors the bold, and I knew in order to be successful that I would have to take risks.

REIMAGINING THE WASTE AND RECYCLING INDUSTRY

Today, Rubicon is the world's largest digital marketplace for waste and recycling. Our mission is to end waste. Because we are a digital company that does not own any trucks or landfills, we can recycle at a higher rate than others that have occupied the space. We fulfill our mission by driving efficiencies in the waste management industry by analyzing data and pairing multinational clients with local, independent waste companies. We are defining a new industry standard where small businesses can be empowered to engage the industry at a more equal level. Rubicon also works to support minority-owned, female-founded, and veteran-led businesses around the country by democratizing national contracts that were previously held captive by just a few large players.

For far too long, big companies dominated our industry. We wanted to give a voice, through our products and services, to independent business owners. The Rubicon platform is our tool for supporting this endeavor. Quite literally, we are entrepreneurs helping entrepreneurs.

Rubicon's solution is simple. About 50 percent of the waste management industry is composed of small, independent haulers and recyclers. These are companies that own their trucks. Rubicon set out to form the world's largest digital waste marketplace, forming a virtual fleet to challenge the status quo of the big players. We are a technology-based company helping small businesses to thrive.

Since its inception, Rubicon has been a transformational company in the waste management industry. We are continuously innovating through research and development and have secured over fifty patents, which we believe will power the reimagined vision of the waste and recycling category. We service everyone from small businesses to enterprise-level Fortune 500 companies in America's premiere cities to work toward a zero-waste business model.

From little more than an idea between two friends and $10,000 worth of credit card debt, Rubicon now has over 8 million unique service locations, a network of over 8,000 haulers, over 8,000 customers, and we operate in all fifty states in the United States in addition to over twenty countries across the world. At the time of the announcement of Rubicon going public, the company was worth nearly $2 billion. It has been an amazing journey—one that could have happened only here in Kentucky.

A SPECIAL THANKS

In addition to my grandparents and my mother, who had to raise me and sacrifice everything, there have been others who have positively impacted my entrepreneurial journey. Brad Kelley, for example, has been a major mentor for many years. He grew up in Simpson County, Kentucky. A lot of people do not realize that he is one of the largest landowners in America. You would never know it from talking to him because he is a humble and private person. Brad is also a great all-around guy.

Brad always pushed me to think big, but he got me to do it in a way that was like an out-of-body experience. The way he spoke was compelling. He did not jump around and shout. Rather, he had a manner of speaking that was like a superpower. His words helped me to achieve the impossible. Consequently, he invested in my business early. To this day, he tells me that he didn't invest in the business; he invested in me.

Other early investors were also critical to the success of Rubicon. Marc Benioff, the founder of Salesforce; Henry Kravis, the co-founder of the investment firm KKR & Co.; and Paul Tudor Jones, the pioneer hedge fund manager were key supporters and champions of my personal success and Rubicon's. To all of those who have helped in this journey to build Rubicon, I am incredibly thankful.

MY ADVICE

The most important piece of advice that I have carried through life came from my mother. She used to always tell me, "You might as well think big because it's free. Even if you end up with a fraction of what you intended to accomplish, you're still better off."

Changing the world through entrepreneurship starts with the right mindset. Think about impact and set out to solve big problems. You must condition your brain to prepare for the opportunities that lie ahead. I don't think anyone is born with large-scale vision and confidence. Those things are learned. Acquaint yourself with doing something on a massive scale and believe that you can make it happen. Dream big and know the best is yet to come.

> "Changing the world through entrepreneurship starts with the right mindset. Think about impact and set out to solve big problems. You must condition your brain to prepare for the opportunities that lie ahead."

DEBBIE SCOPPECHIO

Honorary recollection by husband, Rick Duffy.

Born in Nutley, New Jersey, Debbie Scoppechio grew up in Wappingers Falls, New York and attended Syracuse University before finding her way to Louisville, Kentucky. Debbie was known as a shy young girl who needed to learn how to become more assertive in her early years. Saying that this assessment of her personality would change in her adult years is a massive understatement. Those who knew her best, laugh at the notion that such a version of Debbie ever existed, as she became much more outspoken and forthcoming later in life. In fact, she soon earned the nickname Hurricane Debbie.

After graduating from Syracuse, Debbie went to work for an ad agency out of Buffalo called Faller, Klenk & Quinlan. As a psychology major, she had no advertising experience, but one of the company's founders, Bob Faller, believed in her enough to convince her to come work for the agency. Her years there would become formative not only in her industry experience but also in her polar-opposite transition from introvert to extrovert.

Despite her lack of experience, Debbie adapted instinctively to the advertising world and quickly became known as a young go-getter. After several years of learning from Bob Faller and gaining insights from other colleagues, Debbie acquired an elite skillset that positioned her for bigger and better endeavors.

She left Buffalo for Louisville in 1984 to further her career objectives with Dulaney & K. Shaver agencies. Soon enough, however, Debbie's entrepreneurial spirit wanted to take flight, so she began her own advertising agency with two partners. Later in life, Debbie was noted as saying there were two pivotal moments in her career: Bob Faller believing in her enough to hire her and when her two colleagues convinced her to start a new agency.

The new firm was originally known as Creative Alliance. That name lasted until 2015 when it was renamed Scoppechio by then-Chief Executive Officer (CEO) Jerry Preyss in

Debbie's honor. More recently, the agency became part of a holding company called, OvareGroup.

PRINT ADVERTISING

Creative Alliance was officially founded in 1987. Debbie had fifteen years of ad agency experience at that point. By that time, she had also developed the vision for the values she wanted her company to embody and put forth, which was to put the client first by providing the very best service.

By 1989, the company was billing for about $16 million per year to various local companies. They had a handful of employees but were still missing the big account to take them over the top. That happened when Debbie and her partners landed the print advertising account for Kentucky Fried Chicken (now known as KFC).

KFC was the first national client for Creative Alliance and their first big break. Today, most companies wouldn't spend a ton of money on print advertising, as the digital era has taken over most of that business, but in the late 1980s, print was alive and well. In fact, it was a big part of a company's advertising budget.

Shortly after Creative Alliance won the KFC deal, they were awarded the business for Kentucky Tourism and the Kentucky Lottery. From there, the business took off with revenue and earnings growing consistently for the next twenty-five years and exploding its revenue to around $180 million by 2015.

ACCOLADES AND ACHIEVEMENTS

How did a shy psychology major from the northern part of the country become a wildly successful entrepreneur in Kentucky? Like most entrepreneurs, she took risks, faced challenges, worked hard, and never gave up. She also had an infectious enthusiasm for life and business that spread to everyone around her. It was virtually impossible to not be positively impacted by Debbie's optimism and energy.

When looking back on her career, the skills Debbie picked up as a psychology major likely served her well in business. Some businesses bring in mental health professionals to better serve their staff. Debbie brought this unique skillset with her to understand clients and her employees at a level that other leaders simply could not match.

During her career, she grew a three-person firm to an enterprise-level agency with more than 170 employees and a national footprint, being named as a Top 100 National Independent Agency.

The list of accolades runs long for Debbie Scoppechio. She was named Top Kentucky Woman Business Owner of the Year, the second female inducted into the Kentucky Business Hall of Fame, and Business Leader of the year (Small Businesses) by *Louisville Business First* (journal). She was also given the Heart of the Community Award from Women 4 Women.

Debbie retired in 2015, which was shortly after the company she founded was renamed in her honor. Sadly, she passed away in 2017 after a ten-year battle with metastatic breast cancer. This is where her "never give up" attitude would shine as brightly as possible. Throughout her fight, she maintained a positive attitude and continued to encourage young women to chase their dreams as relentlessly as she did. The shy kid from up north had become a tour de force that emanated to everyone around her throughout the more than three decades she contributed to the business world and the community around her.

ALWAYS A POSITIVE COMMUNITY PRESENCE

A lot of serendipity was involved in Debbie's move to Kentucky, as she gave back substantially to the community throughout her time living and doing business there. Being an entrepreneur meant more than building a business for Debbie; it meant the ability to give back to the people who supported her during her early years of getting started and throughout the many years of her company's tremendous growth. With that in mind, she used her caring and philanthropic nature to do a lot of pro bono work for the city and tourism in the area. She would also do anything to help animals, as she was particularly fond of the creatures who couldn't speak up for themselves.

The people who knew her best would say that behind her nickname of Hurricane Debbie was always a gentle breeze. This was clear when she often held an open checkbook for the causes she cared about most. After being diagnosed with cancer, she gave a lot of money for research and support, especially for children suffering from some form of such a tragic circumstance.

A SPECIAL THANKS

Today, the Scoppechio advertising agency has transformed into OvareGroup, which is a holding company, to assemble a number of unrelated businesses in an attempt to diversify. Despite its modern spectrum of businesses, the company's mission is still driven by the hardworking, client-focused, community-driven energy that Debbie instilled in its founding days. In that way, her legacy in business and the community lives on forever.

A few people were particularly impactful in Debbie's rise to the top of the advertising world in Kentucky and beyond. The first person to make a serious impression was Bob Faller. Bob was the first one to give Debbie a chance in the industry. He recognized her potential despite the fact that she had no experience. Bob Faller was one of her earliest mentors and consequently, someone she respected most of all.

Debbie's integrity was so widely recognized that even the competition respected her. In fact, the CEO of a competing agency, Bob Allison of Doe-Anderson, was considered a good friend throughout Debbie's lifetime. Although they were competitors, Debbie and Bob shared a mutual admiration and respect for each other. Bob thought so highly of his colleague that he said a few words about her tenacious reputation and vibrant personality at her funeral.

Last, David Jones, Sr., who founded the healthcare giant Humana, was another source of inspiration for Debbie. He was always there for her when she sought advice from an experienced and successful professional. He also always sent a note to congratulate Debbie on the many achievements and accolades listed in the previous section. She always appreciated the recognition of people she looked up to like David Jones, Sr., Bob Allison, and Bob Faller.

HER ADVICE

Not long before her passing, Debbie and her husband of many years, Rick Duffy, were granted an interview by local Louisville news affiliate WHAS11. She was battling cancer at the time and continuing her legacy as an entrepreneur and a community presence.

Even with a battle of her own to fight every day, Debbie remained selfless. In addition to her generous donations to assist children with cancer through a partnership with an organization known as Gilda's Club, she also awarded a scholarship every year at the University of Louisville to women pursuing a business career.

Last, she left a powerful quote in that interview with WHAS11, something any aspiring female entrepreneur can take to heart. She said, *"Be the kind of woman who gets out of bed and the devil says, 'Oh crap, she's up!'"*

> "Be the kind of woman who gets out of bed and the devil says, 'Oh crap, she's up!'"

R. DUDLEY WEBB

 I grew up in a small coal mining community situated in Letcher County called Hotspot, Kentucky. Hotspot was a self-operational, unincorporated area of about 300 people. All of the adults there worked for the coal company, which owned and operated the entire camp. They built and owned the housing and ran a commissary that served as the central supply point for the community.

My father was fortunate enough to work outside the mine as a timekeeper and bookkeeper. This position was much preferred to working in the mine for obvious health and safety reasons.

I learned all about simple pleasures in my childhood, as many of my fondest memories in life come from that humble but utterly enjoyable upbringing. One of the highlights of my spare time as a child was simply walking through the woods to collect firewood for our school and bring it back for our potbelly stove. Sports were a lot of fun in Hotspot as well. We had a clay basketball court on the side of a mountain. The problem was that every time the ball rolled over the hill, it would end up in the creek and somebody had to go fish it out. Then, of course, we had a wet ball to play with until it dried out.

Growing up in Hotspot was a unique experience compared to most other places in this country, but it was one that I will forever cherish. If there was nothing else to do, exploring in the woods was always an option. Boredom wasn't really a problem for me, as I was always enamored with building things; I built everything from tree houses to log cabins and all sorts of play structures. I suppose that was foreshadowing things to come.

SCHOOL IN HOTSPOT AND BEYOND

I went to school with about eighty other kids. The schoolhouse had only two classrooms—one was for grades one through four and the other taught kids in grades five through eight. When the students commenced from first grade to second, we moved up one row. That happened each year until we got to the front row and moved to the next classroom for fifth grade.

Commencement from the eighth grade meant we had to get on a school bus and travel to a high school in Whitesburg, Kentucky. That bus ride was an adventure all on its own. It was about forty-five minutes each way, but the route involved some of the roughest terrain I've ever traveled.

The camaraderie between the kids in Hotspot was great. It's been particularly interesting to see the number of kids who came out of such a poor area and attained tremendous success. There were a total of eight or nine kids in my class: one of us went on to work for NASA, another went to the Mayo Clinic, and of course, I did okay on my own as well.

After graduating high school, I attended Georgetown College through the E. O. Robinson scholarship. Georgetown was (and still is) a small, private Baptist school. I enjoyed my time there a great deal, and it was close enough to Lexington that I could occasionally visit and experience what city life was like. Most kids who grow up in a coal mining community aren't so fortunate to do that.

As a freshman, I widened my horizons in life to experience more of this great country. I took summer jobs that showed me some of the most naturally beautiful places America has to offer. My first one was as a fishing guide in Yellowstone

National Park, which was an amazing time of my life. The fish seemed to jump in the boat, while my patrons and I enjoyed a slow and easy ride down the river. I did that for my first two summers in college. The third summer, I got a job teaching golf, tennis, and a few other activities at a honeymoon resort in the Pocono Mountains. That was an interesting fit because I didn't really play tennis or golf, but it was fun and nobody seemed to mind that I wasn't an authority on either subject.

WE CAN'T ALL BE PERRY MASON

Upon graduation from Georgetown College, I went to law school at the University of Kentucky (UK). After three years, I passed the bar and became a solo legal practitioner in Lexington.

Many of the cases in those days were appointed. Most people, especially those who found trouble with the law, couldn't afford an attorney, so the system had to find one for them. Even though those cases weren't exactly set up for success, I knew I had to take just about any case they threw my way. As a private practitioner, I also knew I couldn't afford to sit around and wait for the phone to ring. So I approached as many of the local judges as I could find and asked them to keep me in mind if anything came up.

Sure enough, one of those judges called me one day and

gave me an opportunity. He said, "I'd like to know if you would represent a client in a pro bono deal; it's actually a murder case."

"A murder case!" I thought. "Well, that sounds fine to me. How long do I have to prepare?" He told me, "Well, you can meet the client first, but the trial starts in fifteen minutes."

"Well, I guess that works," I somewhat sheepishly agreed.

Until that day, I thought I was going to be the next Perry Mason. I quickly learned that practicing law wasn't quite as glamorous as the television made it out to be.

My client ended up confessing under my direct examination, so that case was over quick. That's when I decided to make a slight pivot in my career into a real estate practice.

Three years later, my brother Donald, who was also practicing law, joined me in practicing law and buying properties. Eventually, that practice grew to become what is known today as Webb, Hoskins, Brown, & Thompson PSC.

THE RAPID GROWTH OF THE WEBB COMPANIES

Donald and I started small by doing a few closings for various realtors in town. We did a lot of work with deeds. Quickly, we realized that we knew as much as anyone else in town did about real estate. So we grew the business into bigger and better projects. In 1972, we formed The Webb Companies, a consolidation of design, development, finance, legal, construction, marketing, leasing, brokerage, property management, and ancillary real estate functions.

After being fully immersed in the real estate game, I made my first investment in a seven-bedroom property. I flipped and sold it at a decent profit and reinvested it into other properties. I've been enacting the same process in different deal sizes and developments ever since.

My first commercial enterprise was a building formerly occupied by Montgomery Ward's tire store. After I bought the building, a major banker called me and said he wanted the whole block for a development he had planned. He asked me if I would sell it, and I told him that I would if he helped me finance something elsewhere. He agreed and helped me to finance my first bank building. That deal gave us a lot of leverage to develop.

Shortly after, we started building corporate centers, green projects, and many other styles of development, not only in Lexington but from coast to coast and north to south. Our work quickly turned into much higher-profile projects. We partnered with venture capitalists who helped us develop a city block in Austin, Texas. After that, other communities similar in size to Lexington—like Toledo,

Winston-Salem, Raleigh, Durham, and Tampa—called us to build developments that would revitalize their downtown areas.

We've always had a great staff at The Webb Companies and partnered with strong local people with political contacts and financial support. We built this company on the strength, work ethic, and expertise of all those people. Some years, we incurred billions of dollars in new products. Over a period of time, The Webb Companies was one of the largest real estate development groups in the world, with properties from San Francisco to Boston, down to Miami, and numerous points in between.

YOU NEVER KNOW WHERE YOUR LEGACY WILL END UP

Perhaps one of the strangest but most interesting parts of my entrepreneurial journey comes from an iconic photograph taken on a fateful day in September 2001. The following story goes to show that you just never know where your legacy will end up.

At one point, we acquired a dinner cruise chain of boats from Detroit, Michigan. As part of that chain, we built a boat for our personal use called *The Star of America*, and on it, flew an American flag that was purchased from a ship store in Jamestown, Kentucky. It was actually one in a case of flags that we bought for all the boats.

Eventually, we sold *The Star of America* to a couple who docked it in Battery Park, New York. Shortly after the tragedy of 9/11 happened, some firemen were on their way to the wreckage when they spotted the yacht that I sold to that couple. The flag was flying with majestic pride on that boat docked near the World Trade Center.

The firemen grabbed the flag off the back of the boat, brought it to Ground Zero, and raised it as a symbol of America's strength and fortitude. The picture of the three firemen raising it remains one of the most inspirational images of recent American history.

That flag went missing for a while, but it eventually turned up somewhere in the state of Washington. Now it sits in a protective case on display at the National September 11 Museum in New York City.

I'm glad that the flag is where it belongs so people visiting the museum can see it. Hopefully, it acts as a reminder of the greatness of our country for many generations to come.

A SPECIAL THANKS

There were a lot of folks throughout my entrepreneurial journey to whom I owe a great deal of gratitude. For instance, Bill Marriott, Phil Greer, and Jeff Ruby played instrumental roles in getting the City Center Project done for The Webb Companies.

There were also numerous bankers and financiers who believed in what we were doing. Those folks provided the capital we needed to make a difference. Reminiscing about the work we did, I'm fulfilled in the knowledge that we made a difference for the greater good of the local community and across the country. It took a lot of hard work, perseverance, and a willingness to compromise, but we did what we set out to do in the world.

I would be remiss if I didn't mention all the amazing people in Eastern Kentucky who helped me before I invested my first dime in a business.

Recollecting my days as a child in Hotspot, I was fortunate to be raised by honest, hardworking parents who steered me in the right direction. I also had amazing teachers who often didn't have the supplies they needed to effectively help their students learn the material. Rather than give in, they took money from their own pockets and bought what they needed to help the kids.

Fast-forward to today, and I also owe a special thanks to my wife, the former Marla Collins of Versailles (the daughter of former Governor Martha Layne Collins). She has been my biggest supporter since we met. We have twin boys, Alex and Will, as well as a daughter, Ellie. Later in life, our children gave me three wonderful reasons to travel less and focus more on the local community, which is what I have done most in recent years. This allowed me to spend more time with the people most important to me, as well as contribute most effectively to the area I've always thought of as home.

My son Alex is currently working at The Webb Companies part time, Will is in law school and about to take the bar exam, and Ellie is a senior at Georgetown who is enrolling at NYU Law this fall. They've all done well. I'm tremendously proud of them, as well as what The Webb Companies has accomplished over the years.

MY ADVICE

One of my favorite quotes comes from Abraham Lincoln. President Lincoln said, "Show us what should be done and we will find a way." In other words, perseverance is everything. I've always believed that.

The $240 million City Center project we did in Lexington took over ten years to complete. Although it was appropriate and meaningful to the community, we got a lot of pushback from local residents who just didn't like change; they didn't want anything disrupting what they perceived as the way Lexington was and always should be.

All entrepreneurs will encounter resistance when trying to do something they believe in. In fact, if you don't face challenges, you're probably not thinking big enough.

We faced a lot of resistance with that City Center project. The biggest problem was that it was a property designed for mixed usage. In the real estate business, various projects become en vogue while others become unwelcomed, depending on whatever is trending in that given time period. That dichotomy is cyclical in nature. Some years, office buildings are more palatable than others. Some years hotels are seen as signs of prosperity, whereas other years, they're deemed unworthy. Parking garages? They're almost impossible to get approved. Other than those, the popularity and worthiness of various styles of development seem to come and go.

Whenever we hit an impasse with naysayers or people who opposed change, we took those words from our sixteenth President of the United States and persevered. Keep in mind that perseverance doesn't mean what a lot of people think it means. It has nothing to do with stubbornness. Rather, perseverance means having the fortitude to sit down at a table, work together through your differences, and arrive at a compromise that benefits everybody. Perseverance might involve some of the hardest work you'll ever do as an entrepreneur, but it's the only way to push past certain challenges.

All of us at The Webb Companies stuck with that City Center project. Eventually, the stars aligned and it happened. Sure, a little bit of luck was involved, but it was mostly perseverance that got the job done. Now most of the people who live and work in the area are happy to have it there.

If you're an aspiring entrepreneur, my parting piece of advice is to find something you love doing. I'm not talking about opening your world to a chasm of interests; I mean focus on a niche that you really love. By drilling down deep to work on a focus that you're passionate about, you'll never grow old with regret burdening your aging mind.

Loving your work doesn't mean you won't encounter challenges or hard times. If you're going to be successful, working hard is table stakes. But *if you truly love what you're doing, perseverance comes naturally and success is almost sure to follow.*

> "If you truly love what you're doing, perseverance comes naturally and success is almost sure to follow."

CONCLUSION

The Kentucky Entrepreneur Hall of Fame exists to raise awareness of the impact that entrepreneurship has made in the Commonwealth.

In other words, we want Kentucky entrepreneurs to be more famous and feel more appreciated for their contributions.

The second part of our mission is to "encourage others to pursue similarly ambitious endeavors."

If we can share the stories of these successful entrepreneurs, we hope to inspire other Kentuckians to try to follow in their footsteps. Right now, the most famous thing you can be in Kentucky is a basketball player, and while I haven't seen official survey results from around the state about most-sought-after jobs, I can tell you from my experience that my grounded and reasonable parents were hoping I would become a UK basketball player. Turns out my physique wasn't exactly what Tubby Smith was looking for in the early 2000s. I'm hoping the path of entrepreneurship becomes better known and that it becomes one that the next generation of Kentuckians will aspire to take, perhaps just as desirable as becoming a basketball player.

While our mission is and will continue to be to celebrate and inspire Kentucky entrepreneurs, we—meaning myself and the co-founders of the Kentucky Entrepreneur Hall of Fame—selfishly want to learn from these men and women.

This book allowed us to do just that. Let's recap the Kentucky Entrepreneur Hall of Fame Inductees (so far):

CLASS OF 2010

1. **Davis Marksbury**—Exstream Software
2. **Dr. Lee Todd**—Projectron Inc., Databeam
3. **Dr. Pearse Lyons**—Alltech
4. **Jim Host**—Host Communications
5. **John Y. Brown**—KFC
6. **John Schnatter**—Papa Johns
7. **Ralph G. Anderson**—Belcan
8. **Warren Rosenthal**—Jerry's Restaurant, Long John Silvers
9. **William T. Young**—W. T. Young Foods, Overbrook Farm

CLASS OF 2011

1. **Bill Samuels**—Maker's Mark
2. **Dana Bowers**—iPay Technologies
3. **David Jones, Sr.**—Humana
4. **Kent Taylor**—Texas Roadhouse
5. **Wendell Cherry**—Humana

CLASS OF 2012

1. **Bruce Lunsford**—Vencor Ventas
2. **Ronald Geary**—Rescare
3. **Terry Forcht**—Forcht Group

CLASS OF 2013

1. **Bill Gatton**—Bill Gatton Motors
2. **Billy Harper**—Harper Industries
3. **George Fischer**—Metridata Computer, Servend International
4. **R. J. Corman**—RJ Corman Railroad Group

CLASS OF 2014

1. **Chris Sullivan**—Outback Steakhouse
2. **Jim Booth**—Booth Energy Group
3. **John A. Williams, Sr.**—CSI
4. **Junior Bridgeman**—Bridgeman Foods Inc

CLASS OF 2015

1. **George Garvin Brown**—Brown-Forman
2. **Jim Patterson**—Pattco LLC
3. **Jim Thornton**—Thornton's
4. **Phil Greer**—Greer Companies

CLASS OF 2016

1. **Carey Smith**—Big Ass Solutions
2. **"Colonel" Harland Sanders**—Kentucky Fried Chicken
3. **Kent Oyler**—High Speed Access Corp, OPM Services, Inc.
4. **Robert B. Trussell Jr.**—Tempur Sealy

CLASS OF 2017

1. **Doug Cobb**—The Cobb Group, Chrysalis Ventures
2. **Joe Steier**—Signature HealthCARE
3. **Kim Knopf**—Innovative Mattress Solutions

CLASS OF 2018

1. **Don Ball, Sr.**—Ball Homes
2. **Jess Correll**—First Southern National Bank
3. **Jim Headlee**—Summit Energy Services
4. **Joe Craft**—Alliance Resource Partners, L.P.

CLASS OF 2019

1. **Debbie Scoppechio**—Scoppechio
2. **Mike Davis**—Appriss, Inc.
3. **Nate Morris**—Rubicon Global
4. **R. Dudley Webb**—The Webb Companies

To the entrepreneurs in the first book and this one, thank you for the impact you have already made and for the brighter future you are still yet to create.

EMERGING ENTREPRENEURS

The Emerging Entrepreneur Award is presented each year at the Kentucky Entrepreneur Hall of Fame Ceremony to rising entrepreneurs who demonstrate the tenacity, perseverance, and commitment to building his or her company in ways that will impact their industry and community. Often, these founders and their companies are measured against the earlier days of the companies of the Kentucky Entrepreneur Hall of Fame inductees.

Between 2010 and 2019, thirty-three entrepreneurs have been honored publicly with the Emerging Entrepreneur award. Please note that we included the individuals who were recognized from 2015 to 2019 in addition to those rec-

ognized in the first volume of *Unbridled Spirit* to coincide
with the classes of inductees interviewed in this book.

Nate Morris of Rubicon Global became the first entrepreneur to be given the Emerging Entrepreneur award in 2014
and, just five years later, was inducted into the Hall of Fame
in 2019.

The Kentucky Entrepreneur Hall of Fame is proud to recognize emerging entrepreneurs and excited to support them
as they grow their businesses.

YEAR OF RECOGNITION	NAME	COMPANY
2010	Audra Stinchcomb	*Alltranz Inc.*
	Keith Ringer	*Metromojo*
	Randall Stevens	*Archvision, Mersive*
	Ben Self	*Blue State Digital*
	Randy Riggs	*Advanced Cancer Therapeutics*
2011	Wayne Yeager	*Sellathon, Inc.*
	Vidya Ravichandran	*Glowtouch Technologies*
	Zak Boca	*Singlehop, Inc.*
	Heather Howell	*Rooibee Red Tea*
	Rob May	*Backupify*
2012	Brad Wayland	*Bluecotton.com*
	Eric Ostertag	*Transposagen*
	John Williamson	*Ucloser*
	Taylor Trusty	*Blackstone Media*

YEAR OF RECOGNITION	NAME	COMPANY
2013	Drew Curtis	*Fark.com*
	Dave Durand	*Forest Giant*
	April Foster	*Studiocalico.com*
	Matt Wiley	*Bloc Mktg*
2014	Nate Morris	*Rubicon Global*
	Jennifer Mackin	*The Oliver Group*
	Ankur Gopal	*Interapt*
2015	Peter Tower	*Magnolia Photo Booth Company*
	Alex Frommeyer	*Beam Dental*
2016	Tendai Charasika	*SuperFanU*
	Drura Parrish	*Maketime*
	Rebecca Wheeling	*Schedule It*
2017	Twyman Clements	*Space Tango*
	Stacy Griggs	*El Toro*
2018	Gregg Morton	*Fooji*
	Shane Howard	*Custom College Recruiting*
	Alice Shade	*SentryHealth*
2019	Demetrius Gray	*WeatherCheck*
	Jonathan Webb	*AppHarvest*

INVESTORS OF THE YEAR

2016	Chris Young
2017	Bryce Butler
2018	David Goodnight
2019	Mike Schlotman

MENTORS OF THE YEAR

Year	Mentor
2016	George Ward
2017	Elizabeth Rounsavall
2018	Steve Huey
2019	Greg Langdon

THE AWESOME FELLOWSHIP PROGRAM

The Awesome Fellowship is a mentor-driven program designed to accelerate Kentucky's high-tech startups. The program supports startups for up to one year by providing metrics-accountability as well as design, videography, development, legal, and accounting services. Kentucky's emerging entrepreneurs enter into the community through our pipeline of various programs such as the 5 Across Entrepreneur Pitch Competition and Startup Weekend.

From there, they are met with resources and coaching from our community of mentors and investors to vet and support the promising founders and concepts. Those who do particularly well with customer discovery and building a lot from a little get priority when applying to our Fellowship Program.

Unofficially, our Fellowship Program is full of founders who we believe will one day become Emerging Entrepreneurs and go on to become Hall of Famers in the Kentucky Entrepreneur Hall of Fame.

As of August 2022, the fellowship companies have created 527 jobs and raised more than $110,500,000 in outside funding.

The fellowship program provides:

- Access to our network of over one hundred mentors
- Web development, video, and graphic design services
- 24/7 access to Awesome Inc coworking space
- Accountability coaching from the directors of Awesome Inc
- Access to pro bono legal and accounting services provided by Dinsmore & Shohl and DB Virtual Accounting

For more information or to apply, go to https://www.awesomeinc.org/fellowship.

The startup companies in the fellowship by the date of this book's publishing include:

2014 COMPANIES

BlinkScan

Sword

PawnMetrics

YouSawMe

ControlMyADHD

Custom College Recruiting

2015 COMPANIES

MobileServe

Creative Wagering

DonorCentric

ScheduleIt

Travel Notes

ZimmZang

Hippo Manager

Vegy Vida

2016 COMPANIES

Cloverleaf

Credit Fair-E

Inscope Medical

RalphVR

Nymbl Systems

Virtual Peaker

Switcher Studio

FanBloom

2017 COMPANIES

Curio

MyNurse

Meta Construction

Qualmet

Rise Design

WeatherCheck

PASIV Duty

Mailhaven

2018 COMPANIES

Agent Ally

Kare Dental

EZ Turn

FreshFry

TackHunter

Anavii

Podchaser

iReportSource

2019 COMPANIES

Adder

Enable.ai

Moolathon

Toggle Health

EZ Chow

RAADZ

OmniLife

Smart Rotation

2020 COMPANIES

Silver Fern

Pascal Tags

Unitonomy

Forecastr

Job Winner

Casper Security

Nurse CE Central

Hexalayer

2021 COMPANIES

Synaptek

Symba

GoodMaps

Stuccco

Pavr

Borderless

RaveOn

Legal Gantt

2022 COMPANIES

Active Therapy Systems

VRTogether

13 Layers

Inphlu

ACKNOWLEDGMENTS / THANK YOU

This book is a culmination of efforts over more than thirteen years. It has required help from countless people and organizations. Although the following list is far from complete, we did our best to recognize those who have paved the way to make this project possible.

Jay Knoblett for helping us raise our first round of funding.

Nick Such, Justin Raney, and Matt Smith for being the most selfless business partners we could ask for.

Bert Berry for helping start the Kentucky Entrepreneur Hall of Fame as an Awesome Inc intern.

Therese Henrickson for being our first-ever employee at Awesome Inc and sticking with us through the toughest of times.

Jim Gray for writing us our first check to launch Awesome Inc.

Nathan Fort for being with us from the beginning and keeping us organized.

David Caissie and Eliece Pool for helping us stay on track to write this second book.

Gina Greathouse, Bob Quick, Keith Kurzendoerfer, Ryan Hunter, Garrett Ebel, Rachel Swartzentruber, Theresa Simcic, Scott Johnson, Aalap Majmudar, Melanie Stoeckle, Matt Hogg, Lou Allegra, Lee Todd, Jim Host, Elizabeth Rounsavall, Whitney Wallingford, George Ward, Steve Huey, Chris Young, John Williamson, Kyle Lake, David Booth, Drew Curtis, Rick Miller, Brian Poe, Brad Feld, Adam Martin, Mike Sullivan, David McGee, Bryce Anderson, Jamie Pridemore, Marc Nager, Christine McAlister, Thomas Elwood, Stacy Haynes, Tony Ho, Aaron Fons, Pete "The Painter" Dyer, Randall Stevens, Bruce Walcott, Rebecca Fields, Michelle Raney, Mollie Such, Susannah Sizemore, Andy Cox, Calah Ford, Evan Leach, Ryan Copple, John Kiffmeyer, Patrick Kelly, Nolan Lancaster, Seth Ebel, Tommy Crush, Chris Allen, Michael Lewis, Bill Dotson, Jim

Wombles, TW Kinkead, Eric Hartman, Chad Eames, Lee Marskbury, Logan Marksbury, Warren Nash, John Murray, Ann Murray, Keith Raney, Marie Raney, David Such, Patti Such, Stephen Gray, Morgan Franklin, Gary Ditsch, Drew Sutton, Dan Beldy, Steve Pottinger, Jason Jacobson, Jim Ford, Madison Hartung, Tim Williamson, Edward Quinio, Amanda Noel, Brian Mefford, Jason Rainey, David Brock, Anthony Ellis, Lisa Bajournes, Kyle Raney, Peter Briggs, Emily Wehrle, Amanda Murray, Keith McMunn, Zach Frey, Brittany Durham, Katy Brown, Elzaba Anderson, Ross Ladenburger, Jacqueline Benson, Garrett Fahrbach, Justin Hall, Stephen Ruh, Ian Rios, Liz Brown Evans, Mike Hilton, Maggie Bessette, Logan Jones, Jordan Weiter, Heather Seaton, Kerek Plummer, Kevin Mansur, Conner Jones, Camden Sloss, Hannah Eberts, Noah Wilcox, Mackenzie Hanes, Janine Hempy, Josh Stewart, Heath Williams, Elton Cheng, Matthew Gidcomb, Drew House, Reece Walter, Jason Mize, Jonathan Morford, Jacob Hall, David Mitchell, Robert Aldridge, Danny Thorne, Adam Chaffins, Gina Beth Russell, Caleb Cornett, Tommy Warner, all of Team Alpha, and so many more.